The
Joshua
Files

The
Joshua
Files

Matt Bozeat

First published by Pitch Publishing, 2018

Pitch Publishing
A2 Yeoman Gate
Yeoman Way
Worthing
Sussex
BN13 3QZ
www.pitchpublishing.co.uk
info@pitchpublishing.co.uk

A CIP catalogue record is available for this book
from the British Library.

ISBN 978-1-78531-391-2

Typesetting and origination by Pitch Publishing

Printed in the UK by TJ International, Cornwall

Contents

DEDICATION

For my perfect little girl Carla
Diana, Lydia, Mum and Dad
Always in my thoughts Mum

About the author

Matt Bozeat was still at school when he started writing for his local newspaper, the *Northampton Chronicle and Echo*.

He has gone on to work for numerous publications, including *Boxing News* and *Boxing Monthly* and has worked in television for Sky Sports, BT Sport, ITV, Channel Five and Box Nation. He also writes regularly for leading website, Boxing Social.

From Leicester, he lives in Lichfield with his partner Lydia and their young daughter, Carla Diana.

Acknowledgements

Thanks to the following for their time and help – Eddie Hearn, Paul Butlin, Matt Legg, Dorian Darch, Matt Skelton, Michael Sprott, Raphael Zumbano Love, Tommy Gilmour, Andy Brown, Ronald McIntosh, Bob Mee, Declan Johnson, Nick Halling and John Wischhusen. Thanks also to Pitch Publishing and in particular their editorial team of Gareth Davis, Graham Hales and Dean Rockett.

Foreword

I'VE BEEN blessed to enjoy over 40 years in boxing and in that time, I have seen so many wonderful, and sometimes tragic, fighters, fights and events.

No division has provided more of the above than the heavyweight division.

It was 'The Greatest' himself, Muhammad Ali, who lit my burning desire for the sport and the likes of Larry Holmes, Mike Tyson, Lennox Lewis and Evander Holyfield that would keep that flame burning bright as I made my own way in the sport as a boxer and then behind the microphone.

I watched Lennox, sometimes a little too closely, as he rose from Olympic glory to become a dominant world heavyweight champion and to see all that again seemed unlikely.

But along came a youngster who would rise through the amateur ranks to Olympic gold in London and then heavyweight superstardom.

Anthony Joshua has set the boxing world on fire and in this excellent book, my friend Matt Bozeat brings you, from his ringside seat, the punch by punch graphic details of his story, a must read for all boxing and 'AJ' fans as he tells the story from humble beginnings to a fairytale at Wembley Stadium.

This is a terrific book from a true boxing man and the best account of the making of a boxing legend.

Glenn McCrory
(former IBF cruiserweight champion)
February, 2018

Introduction

GROWING UP, boxing didn't interest 'Femi'.

'Never watched it,' said Anthony Oluwafemi Olaseni Joshua, to give him his full name.

He was too busy climbing things!

'As a child, I used to get bored a lot,' Joshua told Sky Sports. 'I remember being bored, always out. I'm a real street kid. I like to be out exploring, that's my type of thing. Sitting at home on the computer isn't really what I was brought up doing. I was really active, climbing trees, poles and in the woods.'

He also ran fast. Joshua reportedly ran 100 metres in 11 seconds when he was 14 years old, had a few training sessions at Callowland Amateur Boxing Club and scored lots of goals on the football pitch.

One season, he scored 43 goals for Kings Langley School in Watford and had trials with Charlton Athletic, but his temper let him down.

'During one game, this guy was trying to wind me up,' remembered Joshua in *The Sun*. 'I got him round the neck and threw him over my shoulder.

'I didn't know my own strength and he didn't land too well. Incredibly, it went to court and I was charged with ABH (Actual Bodily Harm). Luckily, they ended up giving me a slap across the wrist.'

The following year, Joshua got more than a slap on the wrist. He spent two weeks on remand in Reading prison for what he described as 'fighting and other stuff'.

'My dad is a fighter,' revealed Joshua to Sky Sports when asked the roots of his boxing. 'I've heard some stories about my dad. He's a real warrior.

'He is also a real hard worker and I feel that is where I have inherited it from.

'I am my parents and my parents are hard-working people, very strong-minded people, and that's who I am.'

His parents, mother Yeta Odusanya and father Robert, had left Nigeria in their 20s and settled on the Meriden estate in Watford, a town around 20 miles north of London.

Anthony's parents separated when he was still an infant and Yeta took him to Nigeria when he was '12 or 13', apparently intending to move back there.

'I thought I was going there on holiday,' said Joshua, but he found himself being enrolled in a boarding school.

'Every morning we would be woken up at 5.30 and then we had to fetch water,' he said.

'You had to heat the water up by putting a hot iron in it, then you had to make sure all your school clothes were cleaned and ironed.

'The discipline was tough. Sometimes the whole block would just get punished. It might be the cane or you would stand and squat and hold it for 30 minutes. It was tough.

'We got beaten, but that's my culture, beating.'

Joshua said 'I thought I was in heaven' when Yeta took him out of the school and back to Watford and he stayed there with his mother until she moved to London when he was 17.

'It really worked for her,' remembered Joshua, 'but where my heart was, was in Watford.

'I had about five of my aunties and uncles living around the area within a two-minute radius of each other and I did not want to leave the town for any reason, so I asked my aunty if I could stay with her. My mum was happy with it.

'My aunty really looked after me and it got to the point where I left school and thought I was a lot more mature than I was and knew a lot more than I did, so I moved out on my own.

'Living in a room in a hostel, you felt you had nothing to lose.

'In Watford, you have the high street and the bars and the pubs and later at night, the chicken shops.

'Even if you don't drink, people get in your space and it easily kicks off. So yeah, it kicked off a few times and I got arrested.

'I had to relocate to London to get away from all the trouble because the police banned me from the district for a year.'

He moved in with his mother in Golders Green in north London, where the police kept an eye on him.

They fixed an electronic tag to Joshua's ankle to trace his whereabouts and ensure he was where he was meant to be.

'I had to be home at 7.30 every night and it was really tough,' said Joshua, 'but it taught me discipline, it taught me a routine that I never had.

'Being on tag for 13 months meant I had to be home, I had to go and sign in at the station three times a week.

'I had a regimented lifestyle and knew I wanted to put on some size. I wanted to go back to my area looking a lot bigger, a lot stronger, because I wanted to maintain that level of respect that I had, so I started lifting weights.'

He also started a bricklaying course at college and on the insistence of his cousin, Ben Ileyemi, he went to the boxing gym as well.

'He [Ben] brought me down to Finchley [and District] ABC [Amateur Boxing Club], not to train but to watch what he gets up to,' remembered Joshua.

'Me, I chilled out, I sat back and I watched about three sessions, four sessions, something to keep me occupied.

'But I'm a real active person and I went and bought some boots when he [Ileyemi] lent me some money and got involved.'

The coaches at Finchley and District ABC were Johnny Oliver and Sean Murphy.

Murphy looked after Joshua. He was a Commonwealth Games gold medallist in Edinburgh in 1986 and as a professional, he was a heart-on-his-sleeve featherweight who won the Lonsdale belt outright and challenged Steve Robinson for the WBO championship in 1993.

He got into coaching when, against his wishes, his son Danny decided he wanted to box.

Murphy wasn't impressed by his local club, St Albans Amateur Boxing Club, and took Danny to Finchley.

He started helping out with coaching and ended up becoming head coach.

'Nine times out of ten I can tell if someone is going to be any good,' said Murphy. 'Not blowing my own trumpet, but I'll know if they are going to be half decent the first time I take them on the pads.

'And from the first time I took him [Joshua] on the pads I knew there was something, I knew there was something there.

'I never found this out until later on, but he had done a little bit before he had come to Finchley. Not a lot, but he knew he was orthodox and he knew how to stand.

'He always had the perfect build, was mobile and wanted to learn.

'He was a pest, but in a good way. He was always, "Can we do pads? When are we going to do pads? When am I going to spar? When am I going to do this?"'

Joshua remembered his first spar.

'I knew what I was doing until I got in the ring and sparred, and shots were coming in from all angles,' he said. 'I was blowing, it was tough, I didn't have anything.

'But the good thing about it was, as the months went on, I started noticing improvements in my skipping, within my sparring sessions – guys that would run rings around me in the ring, I started running rings around them.'

Murphy said, 'I took him sparring with experienced lads and after a few weeks there wasn't any point because "Josh" was getting the better of them and wasn't learning anything.

'I went to get him registered [to box] in November 2008 and all the other trainers said he wasn't ready to box.

'But they all wanted to train him after they saw his debut!'

That debut was in the function room at the back of The Boston Arms, a pub in Tufnell Park.

'Because I watched a lot of [Mike] Tyson, you never take your eye off your opponent in the corner,' remembered Joshua when interviewed years later by *Boxing News*.

'It's the stare-down. I remember him coming out and me just throwing a one-two and him falling. I thought, "This is all right, this is the hard training." You can imagine how the place erupted.'

That was followed by another knockout win and then Joshua took a fight with Dillian Whyte at a few hours' notice and was beaten on points.

Murphy was still happy with him afterwards. '"Josh" hated losing,' he said. 'He took it very badly.'

Joshua told Murphy afterwards, 'I want to fight him again,' and remembered the loss to Whyte as a turning point. I realised boxing wasn't as easy as I thought,' Joshua said years later. 'So I thought I had to up my level.'

Murphy took a liking to Joshua – he would describe him as 'a big bubbly giant' – and became curious about his life outside the gym.

'When he first come to the gym he was driving a hire car and he had a couple of mobile phones, he never spoke about work,' remembered Murphy.

'I said, "Josh, what's happening? You're getting to quite a good level, and you never speak about work. What's that car out there? Where did you get that? What's that costing?"

'[Joshua said] "It's costing a one [£100] a week."

'"Well, something ain't right if that's the case. You're doing something that ain't right. Stop it. If you don't stop it, you're going to get in trouble."

'He came in a couple of weeks later and he's got a job. He's a security guard. So it's like he realised he was going down the wrong road.'

Joshua stuck with boxing and the next time he took a bout at late notice, this time in Burton upon Trent in the Midlands, he won on points.

'When he came to the ring the crowd went, "Ooooh,"' remembered opponent Frazer Clarke. 'He was a big unit.'

Clarke is not exactly small himself at around 6ft 6in tall and around 16st and had the edge in experience over Joshua.

Named after former heavyweight champion Joe Frazier, Clarke had been part of the Great Britain set-up for a while and earlier that year, he had competed in the European Youth Championships in Poland.

Clarke remembers 'a great little contest between two raw novices' and Joshua won it on a split points decision.

It was a significant success.

'The [England] coaches then came over to me and said, "Where have you been hiding him,"' remembered Murphy.

Joshua kept the momentum going by winning gold at the Haringey Box Cup at Alexandra Palace and the real test would come when he entered the Amateur Boxing Association Championship in 2010.

Every open-class super-heavyweight in the country with ambition would be entered, with the exception of Great Britain Podium squad boxer Amin Isa, and the 2012 London Olympics was in the thoughts of every one of them, including Joshua and Dominic Akinlade, a bus driver from Brixton looking to better himself, and his community, through boxing.

Joshua beat him on points in the London final and was handed byes all the way through to the national final at the York Hall in Bethnal Green, where he met Dominic Winrow, a chunky PE teacher who had piled on a few pounds since representing the Isle of Man at the Commonwealth Games in New Dehli at heavyweight the previous year.

The ABA finals were being filmed by the BBC and a couple of hours before the boxing started, commentator Ronald McIntosh was sitting in a cafe across the road from the venue in the East End of London doing some research when someone started throwing punches at him.

'Joshua was shadow boxing in front of me!' remembered McIntosh.

'He was throwing jabs and rights and then he stopped, burst out laughing and gave me a hug!'

Joshua, it appeared, wasn't one for nerves.

'The first thing I noticed about him when he got in the ring was how composed and assured he was,' said McIntosh.

'Winrow had boxed at the Commonwealth Games, but there was no apprehension from Joshua. He just put it on Winrow and stopped him in the first round.'

The following night, McIntosh spotted Joshua at West Ham United's Upton Park ground, where Kevin Mitchell was challenging hard Australian Michael Katsidis for the interim WBO lightweight championship, and introduced him to BBC radio listeners.

'Anthony Joshua,' McIntosh told listeners, 'remember the name.'

Robert McCracken, performance director for Great Britain Boxing, had made a note of it.

He was there when Joshua beat Winrow and remembered years later, 'There was lots of potential.

'He was a touch raw, but there was real potential. He was brought in for an assessment [with the Great Britain coaches] which tends to happen if you reach the ABA final.'

Joshua impressed enough during his assessment to be called up to the Development squad, the first step towards becoming an international boxer.

Every fortnight, Joshua would train at the English Institute of Sport's boxing facility in Sheffield from Thursday to Monday, training four times every day.

The training was tough and for a while, Joshua wondered if it was for him.

'I was pushed to places that I had never been before,' he remembered, 'places that I thought didn't exist.

'I thought, "This ain't boxing, this is torture."

'I said to myself, "I don't need this in my life right now. I'm happy to stay in Finchley."'

After some thought, Joshua decided to push himself on and made Isa his target.

Joshua believed he had the beating of him and was disappointed when Isa was chosen for the Commonwealth Games in New Dehli in 2010 ahead of him. The reasoning was that Joshua lacked international experience and he knew that if he was to get that experience and become the 'dominant super-heavyweight' the Great Britain coaches were looking for, he had to beat Isa.

Joshua got a shot at him at Liverpool's Echo Arena in November 2010.

The Great Britain Championship gave champions from England, Scotland and Wales the chance to challenge the number one in Great Britain, and on the flip-side, Podium squad members had the chance to cement their position.

The implication here was Joshua and Isa were fighting for Isa's place in the Podium squad.

Beat him and Joshua would get the chance to spend more hours in Sheffield and should he progress, be sent to major championships.

The major championship was the 2012 Olympics, to be held in London. 'There was a lot of talk [about me],' remembered Joshua, 'saying, "This kid, he's got talent, maybe 2016 would be better off for him."'

The walls of the gym in Sheffield were decorated with photographs of previous Olympic medallists.

Audley Harrison and James DeGale gazed down at the fighters as they trained and under 2012 there was a blank silhouette and the words, 'This Could Be You.'

Earlier that year, Isa had lost in the opening round of the Commonwealth Games, indicating he possibly wasn't going to fill that space. From Miguel's Amateur Boxing Club in Brixton, Isa had a fiddly style that was designed to frustrate and draw mistakes from opponents.

Tall and spindly, he switched stances and made it hard for opponents to beat him and those that did beat him seldom looked good in doing so. Joshua didn't find it easy against Isa either when they met in the Great Britain Championship, but he found the answers to score a 6-3 victory on the computers.

It was, he would say later, 'a very, very crucial' win.

Isa dropped out of the Podium squad and though McCracken decided Joshua needed more experience before stepping up, he was well placed to replace him.

Joshua remained on the Development squad with Frazer Clarke, a fighter he had beaten.

Then it all threatened to fall apart.

In March 2011, the police pulled over Joshua while he was driving his Mercedes-Benz on the Grahame Park estate in Colindale, north-west London, and found him with a package containing 8oz of cannabis hidden in a sports bag.

Joshua pleaded guilty to possession, but not guilty to intent to supply and was handed a 12-month community order and told to complete 100 hours of unpaid work. He spent the 100 hours helping elderly people on their allotments 'digging the place up and chopping wood' and helping to grow carrots, tomatoes and courgettes.

Following his conviction, Great Britain banned Joshua from training with them.

Feeling that was harsh, Joshua briefly thought about walking away from boxing before seeing sense. 'I was doing something positive for once, something that I could see a future in,' he said.

The defence of his ABA title gave him motivation, but because of his ban from Great Britain, there were objections from some clubs before, eventually, Joshua was given the all-clear to compete.

He won the London final with a first-round stoppage of Joe Joyce, a future Olympic silver medallist and fine arts graduate, and following two byes, possibly a sign of his growing reputation, Joshua was through to the final in Colchester.

Also there was his cousin, Ben Ileyemi.

He won the ABA heavyweight title with a points win over Stockport & Bredbury ABC southpaw Chris Healey and next in the ring were Joshua and Fayz Abbas, an Iraqi boxing out of Northside Amateur Boxing Club in Manchester, to contest the super-heavyweight final.

Joshua boxed his way to a points win and while he didn't excite the crowd greatly, he did strengthen his position as Great Britain's top super-heavyweight and was getting noticed by professional managers.

He turned down a £50,000 signing-on fee to turn professional, explaining, 'I didn't take up the sport for money, I want to win medals.'

The Great Britain coaches thought he had a chance of winning medals. They lifted Joshua's ban, called him up into the Podium squad and sent him to the European Championships.

'The first time I met him,' remembered McCracken, 'I thought he was too good to be true.

'Here was this big, athletic fella who was a good fighter and a nice guy too. But it turned out he was everything he seemed to be.'

McCracken had been a good fighter himself.

One of three boxing brothers from Birmingham – Spencer and Max were also professionals – McCracken won a silver medal at the World Cup in Dublin in 1990 and also that year, he reached the last eight of the Commonwealth Games in New Zealand.

McCracken would later say he regretted turning professional at 22 years old rather than staying as an amateur and targeting the Barcelona Olympics in 1992, but he went on to have a good career under manager Mickey Duff. A textbook, stand-up boxer, McCracken won the British light-middleweight and Commonwealth middleweight titles and was beaten in 11 rounds by Keith Holmes in a challenge for the WBC middleweight championship at Wembley Arena in 2000.

He went on to coach Mick Hennessy's stable of fighters, including Carl Froch, and in 2009, his former Great Britain coach Kevin Hickey asked him and Richie Woodhall, a bronze medallist at the 1988 Seoul Olympics, to give advice to the Great Britain amateur squad.

Woodhall was also training professionals at the time and with amateur boxing matches being switched from four two-minute rounds to three three-minute rounds and a more professional feel, Hickey reckoned their input could be vital.

McCracken went on to take the post of performance director with Great Britain Boxing and his job was to deliver Olympic medals in London.

Millions of pounds of public money, via UK Sport and the National Lottery, was poured into producing medallists, but still, the job was a tough one.

James DeGale and David Price had turned professional after winning medals at the 2008 Beijing Olympics, along with fellow Olympian Billy-Joe Saunders and world amateur champion Frankie Gavin, leaving McCracken to rebuild.

He clearly saw something in Joshua and set about reshaping him.

'I have always been tall,' said Joshua, 'but my idol at the time was, and still is, Mike Tyson, who is a short guy, stocky. I'm taller, thinner, rangier.

'I used to think I was Mike Tyson and boxed short, tucked up, and they [the Great Britain coaches] told me,

"That's not the way you're going to win these fights as an amateur. You need a hit-and-don't-get-hit type of boxing style."

'So they completely changed me and put me in with experienced fighters sparring-wise. I got hit hard, I trained, I learnt in the gym, which is the best place to do it.'

McCracken was impressed by Joshua and wanted to see how he would fare in the forthcoming European Championships in Turkey.

After his ban was lifted, Joshua only had ten days to prepare for what was a very different challenge. The ABA Championship was spread over a couple of months, while major internationals, such as the European Championship, were all over within a week or so, meaning boxers could be fighting almost every day.

The idea was to see how Joshua dealt with that, along with the travel and the tougher competition ahead of the World Championship in Azerbaijan later that year.

Joshua dealt well enough with his first two opponents in Ankara, beating Germany's Eric Brechlin and Cathal McMonagle from Ireland, and his third bout in four days was a quarter-final against Romanian southpaw Mihai Nistor.

Joshua would later admit that by then, he was feeling tired.

Still, he boxed well enough against Nistor, a left-handed version of Mike Tyson according to the excitable Romanian press, to be ahead on points going into the third and last round.

Early in the third, Nistor got outside a slow Joshua right hand and slung a sweeping southpaw left hand that crashed on to Joshua's chin and stiffened his legs, forcing the referee to give him an eight count. On the resumption, Nistor went for broke and Joshua tried to hold. Nistor connected again with Joshua's jaw, flinging him into the ropes and after the referee had counted to eight, he waved the fight off.

McCracken was happy enough. 'He boxed three times in four days and you could see the potential was there [to do well],' he said, 'once he had got fit and had a bit of know-how at international level.'

Joshua blamed the loss on being 'knackered' and knuckled down.

'The training [at Great Britain] doesn't suit every boxer,' Woodhall told me at the time. 'You're away from home and it's full-time training.

'But Anthony loves every minute of it. You couldn't ask for a better pupil.'

Woodhall described Joshua as 'a sponge', explaining, 'He retains every bit of information you give him,' and he worked hard.

The coaches would tell Joshua what he needed to work on and the following day, there would be an improvement.

Joshua would spend his evenings in front of his mirror practising before getting up early for the next day's training.

He would be weighed at around seven o'clock every morning and that was followed by track and strength and conditioning sessions.

The afternoon was spent resting ahead of a three-hour gym session when the boxers would spar and work on their technique.

The coaches saw enough progress in Joshua to send him to the World Championship in Azerbaijan, a decision described as 'a gamble' by Woodhall, and if he reached the semi-finals there, he would qualify for the Olympics.

Given that he was ranked at 47 in the world by the Amateur International Boxing Association [AIBA] and the super-heavyweight division was unusually competitive, that seemed unlikely.

'He developed at a fast rate,' remembered McCracken, 'but did we think he was going to reach the final in Azerbaijan?

'Possibly not, no. But we got his temperament right, so he believed in himself.'

That self-belief revealed itself when *Boxing News* interviewed Joshua ahead of the World Championship.

'History is calling for a great heavyweight right now,' declared the 47th best amateur in the world, a novice of around 30 bouts.

The confidence was still there when Joshua got to Azerbaijan.

'You would get boxers,' said McCracken, 'who say, "What's my draw?" and he [Joshua] was different in how he took the draw.

'It was completely irrelevant to him. He didn't mind drawing the Cuban or the Russian first up. Not a problem to him. That still stands out for me and I haven't really come across that with any other senior boxer.'

If there was a fighter to avoid in the draw in Azerbaijan, it was surely Roberto Cammarelle, a 31-year-old Italian southpaw who had won the previous two World Championships and Olympic gold in Beijing three years earlier. The gulf between Joshua and Cammarelle was such that had Joshua beaten Nistor in the European

Championships, the Great Britain coaches would have pulled him out rather than let him face Cammarelle in the semi-finals.

They met in the quarter-finals of the World Championship and at stake was a place at the London Olympics.

Cammarelle was a seasoned boxer who had developed a style that won fights at the highest level.

He would stand in front of opponents with his hands low, inviting them to punch him, make them miss with a twist of his body and quickly pounce with counter punches. No counter punch he ever threw was better than the crunching left hand that toppled Chinese giant Zhang Zhilei in the Olympic final in Beijing in 2008.

Though Joshua was a novice by comparison, Great Britain coaches felt that if he stuck to the game plan they had drawn up, it was a fight he could win. The strategy was for Joshua to keep the fight at long range and make Cammarelle come forward and walk on to punches.

Joshua followed the strategy well enough to be in touch at 6-5 behind after the opening round. Cammarelle got on the front foot in the second round and, just as the Great Britain coaches planned it, he ran on to right hands.

Joshua was 11-9 up going into the last round and there was a big drive from Cammarelle in the last three minutes. There wasn't much between them as they slugged it out, but the judges didn't think Cammarelle landed enough punches to overturn the two-point deficit.

Joshua won 15-13, though Cammarelle looked unhappy with the decision.

McIntosh described Joshua's win as 'one of the most significant results by a home nations boxer for years.

'There was such a disparity in experience between them. For a novice like Joshua to beat a boxer of that quality really was outstanding.'

The 47th best super-heavyweight was, against all the odds, going to the Olympics and given who he had beaten to get there, he had to have a chance of winning a medal.

'It [beating Cammarelle] showed me that as long as I stayed amateur, these guys have nothing on me,' said Joshua later.

'No fear, I can compete with them. Whether we're boxing or trading, I can compete with them. He [Cammarelle] is someone I actually looked up to as an amateur and to compete with him and beat him gave me a real boost of confidence.'

Joshua wanted to go to the Olympics as the world champion.

He won his World Championship semi-final inside a round, Germany's Eric Pfeiffer being ruled out with a broken nose, but had to fight more than his opponent in the final.

Magomedrasul Medzhidov had the Azerbaijan crowd, around 800 soldiers and the country's president behind him when he fought Joshua.

He could also match Joshua for size and strength. 'I'd never boxed someone that strong,' said Joshua after a 22-21 points decision went against him following what *Boxing News* described as 'a roaring' contest.

The Great Britain coaches felt that had the fight been held anywhere other than Azerbaijan, the decision would have gone Joshua's way.

Joshua wept all the way to his changing room, but when he looked back on it months later, he remembered the thrill of the fight.

'I really enjoyed that fight in the final,' he remembered in a *Boxing News* interview with John Dennen.

'It was a crowd-thrilling fight. It really tested me, my endurance, my heart, my chin, where I'm at technically.

'There was nowhere to hide in that ring. It was all or nothing.'

* * * * *

THE British press wanted to know all about this 21-year-old from Watford and whether he could be the nation's next heavyweight hero.

Joshua would admit that at first, he found this interest in him unsettling.

Only Dennen, the amateur editor of trade paper *Boxing News*, had covered him previously and now the national press were quizzing him about his past and becoming experts on his future.

Not only that, for the first time since he started boxing four years earlier, there was real pressure on Joshua.

'It's not something people were drilling into my head, "You're going to be an Olympic champion, you keep on working hard and you're going to go to the Olympics,"' he remembered.

'It was trial and error. "Let's send him to this tournament and see how he does – oh he's won it! Let's send him to this tournament and see how he does. Let's send him to the World Championships and see how he does." It was all about trial and error.'

The British boxing team was strong in London. Thomas Stalker captained a team that also included Andrew Selby, Luke Campbell, Josh Taylor, Fred Evans, Anthony Ogogo and Joshua.

The fighter they were all talking about was Joshua. By now, he had studied enough boxing to understand both what he called the public's 'fascination' with heavyweights and the division's history.

He told *Boxing Monthly* ahead of the Olympics, 'I hope to be one of those people that everyone looks up to and says, "Remember Joshua and what he done."

'I think about Lennox [Lewis] and [Muhammad] Ali and I want people to think of me like that.'

Joshua was keen to connect with his public, personally replying to good-luck messages from fans on social media in the build-up to the Olympics, and Woodhall said, '"Josh" always has time for people and can be a massive star like Frank Bruno.

'But he has to forget about how famous he can be. He has to stay focused on winning that gold and he has the tools to do it. "Josh" is a good mid-to-long-range boxer and when he finds his rhythm he's very hard to beat. He's got power and sticks to the game plan. He doesn't get involved when he doesn't need to.'

His draw in London was tough.

Erislandy Savon was a 6ft 5in Cuban who was mobile and had boxing in his DNA.

His uncle, Felix, won heavyweight gold at three Olympics, between 1992 and 2000, and along with Savon, Joshua also had to deal with the pressure of the occasion.

The Olympic boxing was held at the ExCel Arena in London's Docklands and Joshua would later admit that when he fought Savon, he thought rather too much about shutting out the crowd, tightened up and struggled to let his hands go.

He got away with it – just.

The judges had Joshua winning 17-16, a decision not popular with everyone who saw the fight, but the system of scoring fights was as reliable as it ever had been.

Three of the five judges sitting at ringside had to register a punch 'instantaneously' for it to register.

'I put my hands up,' said Joshua a year or so later, 'it wasn't my best performance.'

That set up a quarter-final against Zhang Zhilei, the giant Chinese southpaw who had won silver behind Cammarelle in Beijing four years earlier.

Joshua says he 'found his mojo' during a 15-11 points win. 'I got my groove back from my first fight,' he said, 'and I was on a roll.

'But I didn't let it get to me, I didn't get too overwhelmed. I still wasn't happy because I had a long way to go. I still had some tough fighters in my draw.'

The win meant Joshua was guaranteed to win a medal and if he beat Ivan Dychko in the semi-final, it would be either silver or gold.

Dychko was a towering 6ft 9in boxer from Kazakhstan who Joshua knew well.

He had sparred him shortly after joining the Great Britain squad a couple of years earlier and found it tough.

He remembered Dychko as 'a really slick boxer, really rangy.

'But I was so determined to beat him. I did not stop applying that pressure.'

The pressure earned him a 13-11 points win and a place in the Olympic final.

'The job's not done yet,' Joshua said ahead of his 43rd amateur bout. 'I want that gold medal.'

To get it, he would have to beat Cammarelle again.

The tactics were the same as they had been in Azerbaijan ten months earlier.

Joshua stood off, moved to his left and looked to walk Cammarelle on to right hands. Until the final 30 seconds of the round, it worked. Joshua found himself pinned in a corner towards the end of the session and took enough punches for the judges to have Cammarelle 6-5 ahead after the first round.

'JOSH-U-A!' chanted the London crowd during a cagey second round of mostly feints and jabs and at the bell, Cammarelle had stretched his lead to three points at 13-10.

'The coaches told me, "'Josh' you're three points down!" he remembered.

'I said, "Come on, I'm not three points down." Because sometimes they tell you these things when you're doing well and they don't want you to get too ahead of yourself.

'So I was like, "Are you being serious? I'm three points down?"

'Before the bell went [for the last round] my legs were burning and I said to myself, "This is the last fight I'm going to have as an amateur if I decide to turn professional, why not put everything on the line?"

'I didn't want to go out and make it a war and end up getting caught myself, so I thought, "Still box, keep it clever, but back up Cammarelle and give him something that he has never had before."

'So we were trading shots, we're boxing, we're moving and I came back to the corner after a tough three minutes and the judges said, "We have seen this as a draw."'

The scores were 18-18 after a strong finish from Joshua and the bout would be decided by countback.

That meant the number of button presses by all five judges were counted up and the highest and lowest scores would be discounted.

Joshua was ahead 56-53 and the gold medal was his.

The Italians protested, but the decision stood and Britain had a new boxing hero.

Joshua was awarded the MBE and a post box on Watford High Street was painted gold to commemorate his achievement.

'I could have been a stereotype,' said Joshua, 'a young kid getting into trouble. It just shows you can achieve anything and you can really change your life. I feel honoured to be involved in boxing.'

* * * * *

'I'M the champ, what's next?" thought Joshua. 'I've got to climb to the top of another mountain now.

'I've got to put everything that I have achieved over the last three years as an amateur behind me. What is next? Am I going to turn professional? If I turn professional, what type of fights am I going to be in? Should I stay on as an amateur and gain valuable experience? Keep on honing my skills under the radar, potentially compete in the Commonwealth [Games], the Worlds [Championship], Europeans, 2016 [Olympics]?

'What should I do next?

'I went around, I searched high and low, travelled to different countries and met different people, exchanged e-mail with people all over the world, Ukraine and Russia, went to Jamaica, LA [Los Angeles] to just really get some advice and I met [former world cruiserweight and heavyweight champion] David Haye, spoke to Rob McCracken and all the GB team individually before I made my final decision.'

The rumour was, once he had recovered from a foot operation, Joshua would turn professional with Los Angeles-based Golden Boy Promotions, headed by Oscar De La Hoya, the brilliant former six-weight world champion.

But on the advice of McCracken, he agreed a three-year deal with Matchroom instead.

'They match their fighters tough, they give all their challengers about ten weeks' notice so they can prepare to the best of their capability and they have got Sky behind them which is a great platform,' he explained.

'They have got so many dates so I can just keep on perfecting my skills, keep on boxing.'

Joshua trusted Matchroom – 'They are straight up,' he said – and liked their boxing chief, Eddie Hearn.

Hearn was an engaging character who, like Joshua, always thought big.

Hearn fell for boxing when, aged eight, he sat ringside at his father's first boxing promotion.

On the advice of his mother, Barry Hearn became a chartered accountant – 'I've never seen a poor one,' she told her son after returning from a day's work cleaning houses – and on the advice of his accountant, he invested the money he made in a chain of snooker clubs.

'Six months after I bought the billiard halls, the BBC started showing lots of snooker on television,' remembered Hearn. 'I was very lucky – and I've always said it's better to be born lucky than be born good looking.'

The player who dominated snooker during its boom years in the 1980s also happened to be a Hearn discovery.

'I met Steve Davis when he was 18 years old,' remembered Hearn. 'He didn't have any personality, but he had a steely-eyed determination.

'Steve was a total machine.'

He would dominate snooker during the 1980s, hoovering up six world titles, and Hearn moved on to boxing.

His first show was a co-promotion with Terry Lawless and was an impressive statement of intent. There were 40,000 fans at White Hart Lane in October 1987 to watch a fight between Frank Bruno and Joe Bugner that, with the help of the tabloid press, sold rather better than it might have done.

Bruno was a national treasure, a strong but vulnerable fighter whose dashed-hopes story chimed with millions, and though Bugner had been the distance with Muhammad Ali (twice) and Joe Frazier, he remained a villain in the eyes of the British public for sending Henry Cooper into retirement with a controversial points win in March 1971.

'What happened to me after that fight was worse than being crucified,' remembered Bugner. 'I was blamed for something I had no control over and one moronic Labour MP even called for me to be stripped of my title, stripped of my assets and sent back to wherever I came from.'

Bugner went on to emigrate, reinvented himself as 'Aussie Joe', and to the fury of the British public, he returned at the age of 37 with the intention of beating Bruno, 12 years his junior.

Predictably enough, Bruno won convincingly in eight rounds and there watching every punch at ringside was Eddie Hearn.

'After that, I was always around the gym,' said Hearn, who showed promise as a cricketer in his teens. 'I would get the bus to Romford after school and see people like Herbie Hide and Eamonn Loughran training.'

His father found his biggest success with Chris Eubank.

Eubank was an eccentric showman who wore a monocle, talked eloquently on many subjects and was hard to his core.

He was a WBO middleweight and super-middleweight champion and most of his 24 world title fights, a record for a British boxer, were under Barry Hearn's Matchroom banner on ITV.

In his teens, Eddie Hearn – or rather 'Eddie Hills' – fought himself, as an amateur with Billericay Amateur Boxing Club.

'They introduced me as "Eddie Hills" and I was devastated,' said Hearn.

'I told my dad and I found out it was all his idea. He thought if they knew who I was, they would really put it on me and take liberties.

'I had some skills, I fancied myself a bit, I thought I was Sugar Ray Leonard, but you can't be a fighter if you grow up in a nice house and go to public school.

'The other lads were much tougher than me.'

Hearn – or Hills – still won all three bouts before a sparring session convinced him his future lay elsewhere.

'When I was 15, they put me in to spar a lad of 18 or 19 and he gave me a pasting,' he said. 'I was miles behind him – and he wasn't a world beater. I don't think I went back after that.

'I left school and went to work for a sports management and marketing company in the West End.

'I was representing golfers on the US and PGA Tour. I did that for six or seven years.

'I decided to work at Matchroom and started on golf and went on to online gaming, producing online poker tournaments.

'I was at the World Series of Poker in Las Vegas and Audley Harrison was at my table. He asked me to get him a six rounder, but I talked him into "Prizefighter".'

'Prizefighter' was an eight-man tournament that offered fighters at opposite ends of their careers the chance to move forward with three wins on the same night. 'Prizefighter' offered exposure to prospects on the way up and a possible way back for older fighters like Harrison, a 2000 Olympic super-heavyweight champion who had fallen disappointingly short of the lofty expectations he had from himself.

'I told him if he won "Prizefighter" then he could fight Albert Sosnowski for the European title and David Haye for the world title,' said Hearn.

'I just made it up, but everything I promised I delivered and I learned a lot along the way. I didn't really know what I was doing.

'The Haye–Harrison fight didn't really deliver [Harrison barely landed a punch before being beaten in three rounds] and I took the flak.

'I was in a sandwich shop and I remember everyone looking at me as if to say, "We want our money back."

'After the Haye fight I thought, "That's me done." I didn't have any ambitions to be a boxing promoter. I just wanted to have fun and make a few quid.

'But a couple of weeks later, [coach] Tony Sims contacted me and said, "Do you want to look after Darren Barker?"

'Then I met Kell Brook at a "Prizefighter" in Liverpool and he said his contract with Frank Warren was coming to an end. We met him and signed a contract.

'A couple of weeks later Rob McCracken rang and asked if I wanted to work with Carl Froch.

'It really did happen that quickly.

'In the space of a couple of months we signed up Barker, Brook and Froch and then other fighters wanted to get on board.'

This put Hearn in a strong position – and it became stronger after he convinced Sky Sports that they should only screen Matchroom shows.

Four promoters – Matchroom, Frank Warren, Frank Maloney and Ricky Hatton – shared 40 shows on Sky Sports between them every year.

The shows were on Friday nights and were topped by a fight for a major title, British, Commonwealth, European or world, and lasted for two hours.

Frank Warren broke away to set up his own subscription channel, Box Nation, in 2011, Mick Hennessy had a handful of TV dates with Channel Five and, unhappy with the ratings for many of their boxing shows, Sky Sports had a rethink.

They were thinking of having fewer shows and investing more in them.

Hearn made his move.

He says the turning point was the Kell Brook–Matthew Hatton fight at the Sheffield Arena in March 2012.

'Nobody had done an arena fight for a while and we sold 9,000 tickets,' he said.

'That fight was the turning point.

'I think promoters had become lazy and thought, "Sky will put up with a Commonwealth title fight topping the bill and an eight-round chief support." That fight showed there was a market for big shows. Sky looked at boxing and thought, "This could work."

'There were four promoters battling each other and it was a mess.

'I told Sky they should give us all the boxing shows, but there should be fewer shows and they should spend more money on them.

'You can't put on quality boxing every week like they were trying to, it just doesn't work.

'Sky had a good relationship with Matchroom through the darts and other sports and eventually they agreed and gave us a two-year deal.

'The deal was 20 shows plus four pay-per-views and that meant we could grow the team.'

There were now only two major promoters in Britain, Hearn and Warren, and Joshua chose Hearn.

Given the chance to create a boxer, Hearn would have created Joshua.

Here was a charismatic heavyweight who was already a national hero after winning Olympic gold in London.

Joshua could appeal to an audience beyond hardcore boxing fans – and that was the audience Hearn was chasing.

That Olympic gold was no guarantee of success in the professional ring, as Harrison had proved, but it gave Joshua a good grounding to build on with his trainer, Tony Sims.

Best known for working as Carl Froch's cuts man and steering Darren Barker to the IBF middleweight championship, Sims, whose own boxing ambitions were effectively ended when he became a father at 18, was most proud of his association with Lee Purdy.

Purdy turned professional with only a handful of unlicensed fights behind him and with Sims in his corner, he won the British welterweight title and fought in Atlantic City.

Nick Halling remembers Joshua meeting the press at Sims's gym in Essex, shortly after he signed with Matchroom.

Halling described the gym as 'a really grotty, spit and sawdust place, not the sort of place you want to take your grandmother', and was there to talk to Barker and John Ryder as research for his job as boxing commentator with Sky Sports.

'I heard Joshua was coming, so I thought I would hang around and introduce myself,' said Halling.

Joshua kept him hanging around.

'On this occasion he was only half an hour late and as I found out later, that was quite good for him,' said Halling.

'If Anthony is supposed to be somewhere at two o'clock, he will be there closer to four.'

Halling remembered that when Joshua did turn up, he made an instant impression.

'He had a real aura about him,' said Halling. 'He was a big specimen with a big, warm smile and he made a point of going around the gym, shaking everyone's hand.

'He didn't know who I was, I might have been the cleaner for all he knew, but he still made a point of shaking my hand and saying, "Hi, I'm Anthony, nice to meet you."'

Everyone who met Joshua seemed to be impressed.

Sky Sports proudly unveiled him on their weekly *Ringside* magazine show and Bob Mee, boxing historian and author, sat next to him. 'He didn't seem consumed by his ego,' said Mee.

'He seemed grounded or as grounded as it's possible to be when you're the Olympic champion and people are throwing lots of money at you.

'He accepted that he was a novice, that he had a lot of developing to do. His attitude seemed to be, "I won the Olympics, but so what? That's in the past."

'He knew where he was.

'He seemed to like people as well. He wanted to connect.'

* * * * *

Anthony Joshua didn't let me down.

The choice was to either bring this book out before he fought Joseph Parker – or afterwards.

I chose afterwards, knowing victory for Parker would undo years of my work.

Not many were predicting that outcome, certainly not the bookmakers, but there were those who felt Joshua may have to come through a crisis or two to beat the New Zealander.

Parker was also an undefeated world champion – he held the WBO belt – and was known as a fearless, quick-fisted fighter who could box and punch.

Frazer Clarke was well placed to pick a winner of the first heavyweight unification fight between unbeaten champions seen in Britain. He sparred around 70 rounds with Joshua in the build-up to the fight and further back, he lost a points decision to Parker.

Clarke, preparing for the Commonwealth Games, reckoned this would be a tactical fight – and Joshua would win. Joshua said much the same.

He wrote in his *London Evening Standard* column on the eve of the fight of being 'a 12-round fighter' and rather than predicting an explosive confrontation, he wrote about the virtues of footwork, timing and counter-punching.

Both were light at the weigh-in. Joshua scaled 17st 4¼lbs, his lightest since he beat Michael Sprott in November 2014, and Parker was 16st 12½lbs.

Joshua was also a couple of inches taller, had a longer reach and that, said his coach Robert McCracken, would be decisive. He revealed the game plan was to 'use the reach to dominate' – and though not everyone in the crowd enjoyed watching it, that's what Joshua did.

For most of the 12 rounds, Joshua was able to impose himself on Parker and keep him on the outside with his jab. Parker flicked out flurries of fast jabs in the opening few rounds, but mostly they hit Joshua's arms and gloves or fell short and when Joshua jabbed, he usually landed and his feet kept the New Zealander under pressure.

Joshua was careful because, with his head movement and hand speed, Parker was always dangerous on the counter should he miss and in the fifth and sixth, the New Zealander got on the front foot and took a few more chances.

Joshua was untroubled by his rushing attacks, but still, there was some concern in his corner ahead of the eighth.

He responded by racing to the centre of the ring at the start of the round and putting Parker back where he wanted him, on the perimeter of the ring where he could hit Parker and the New Zealander couldn't hit him back.

There was some drama in the tenth when Joshua caught Parker with his elbow during a tangle on the ropes and sliced open a cut on his left eye, but Joshua stuck to the game plan and jabbed his way to victory.

Sections of the crowd booed – they had come to see a knockout – but McCracken rated Joshua's performance 'nine out of ten'.

Twenty-one fights into his career, Joshua had the WBA Super, IBF and WBO heavyweight belts – and that left only WBC champion Deontay Wilder to beat ...

Fight No 1
Emanuele Leo

At: The O2 Arena, Greenwich, London

On: Saturday, 5 October 2013

Opponent's record: Fights 8 Wins 8 Losses 0

Joshua's weight: 16st 6.75lb

Opponent's weight: 16st 6.5lb

Scheduled for: 6 Rounds

Result: Joshua won by first-round stoppage

JOSHUA WAS going to start his professional career against Paul Butlin at the O2 Arena – but Emma Bainbridge would not have stood for that.

Saturday, 5 October happened to be the day she was going to become Mrs Paul Butlin and the offer to fight Joshua was politely declined.

Eddie Hearn and his team had to look elsewhere for an opponent and it wasn't an easy job. 'We couldn't just bring in some fat Hungarian,' said Matchroom's then head of boxing, John Wischhusen. 'Joshua was an Olympic champion and the opponents had to look the part early on.'

Matchroom weren't looking for another Mike Middleton, the part-time private investigator with the losing record thrown to Audley Harrison on his professional debut after he won super-heavyweight gold at the 2000 Sydney Olympics.

Wischhusen found someone who Hearn would later describe as 'the perfect opponent'.

Emanuele Leo was a 32-year-old from Italy known as 'The Colossus of Cupertino' and had won all eight of his professional fights, three of them inside the opening round.

Pitting a debutant against an 8-0 prospect appeared to be a huge risk, but what looked a tough fight for Joshua was really a tough fight for Leo.

The whisper was, even those close to the Italian weren't that excited about his future after watching him build his record against novices and journeymen, while Joshua was shining in the gym.

'I've seen a lot of heavyweights come and go,' said Wischhusen, 'and Joshua wasn't big and lumbering, like lots of them are.

'He was an athlete, quick and he punched very, very hard.'

Leo was unbeaten, so would come with ambition, take chances and, given the likely gulf in class between them, the likelihood was, he would get knocked out.

Perfect for Joshua's debut.

Looking ahead to his professional career, Joshua told *Boxing News*, 'First year, they can match me with any opponent. I've just got to take it as a learning stage.

'I've got to remember I'm not competing with Wladimir Klitschko or no one like that yet, you know what I mean?

'I can't put myself under too much pressure because I'm not competing for my Olympic title just yet. Definitely I want to take it serious, but I'm not going to put too much pressure on myself because I know that [the opposition] is not the best in the world just yet.

'When I signed up to my first fight, I was looking at it maybe as a four-year period, an apprenticeship, before I try to compete for my [new] Olympic medal, a professional title. But who knows?

'I don't want to keep talking world titles just yet, but do you see, it is kind of like the same procedure.

'If fame comes I'm going to be okay with it. I don't want to be hyped up and made out to be something I'm not. The Olympics didn't satisfy me. I have a lot more to achieve.'

The aim, Joshua said upon turning professional, was to become a millionaire through boxing.

'I think the hunger for success came from a young age,' he explained. 'I really looked up to my dad growing up. They call him "Big Josh", "Big Guy". I've seen him with big gold chains, owning properties and motorbikes.

'I've seen all this growing up and what you see growing up is what you want to do as you get older.'

Joshua told the *London Evening Standard* ahead of his debut that he was reading a book called *Think and Grow Rich* and playing chess.

He liked the moves and the counter moves on the chess board. 'A boxing match can be a bit like chess,' he said.

Joshua, as all fighters do when they make the switch from amateur to professional boxing, told the press and himself that the paid code suited him rather better.

He liked the feel of the smaller, tighter gloves worn by professionals, weighing 10oz rather than 12oz.

'I tried on some 10oz gloves,' Joshua said days before his debut. 'You could break down a brick wall with those.'

The atmosphere in the changing room at the O2 Arena he shared with his cousin Ben Ileyemi, also making his debut on the show, was relaxed.

'Considering all the pressure he's under, he was really calm,' said Tony Sims, 'as calm as you have ever seen a fighter.'

Joshua would later admit there were nerves 'because I wanted to perform at my best. The nerves were flowing, the butterflies were tingling. I had been out of the ring for a while and wanted to capture a knockout.'

Sky Sports built the expectation, introducing a show that included Bury's honest Scott Quigg defending his WBA super-bantamweight championship against Cuban Yoandris Salinas as 'launch night for Olympic gold medallist Anthony Joshua', and there was a feverish excitement around the arena when the crowd got their first glimpse of him.

Joshua acknowledged as many supporters as possible on the way to the ring, smiling, bumping fists and waving. He was, according to master of ceremonies John McDonald, 'the future people's champion'.

Once the fight got under way, early impressions of Joshua were impressive. He was good on his feet, half stepping in and out of range, and his punches were fast, while by comparison, Leo looked very much a novice. The guard was wide, his chin was high and he squared his feet up when he rushed in.

Joshua caught him, not quite flush because his timing wasn't quite there after so long out of the ring, on the way in with a right hand, but didn't follow up. There was no hurry. Joshua sensed there would be more openings soon and when he spotted one midway through the round and put his punches together, Leo grabbed.

As referee, and former good professional, Ian John-Lewis moved in to disentangle them, Leo shaped to throw a right hand. 'I just saw him flinch,' remembered Joshua, 'and I just wanted to make sure before he landed anything on me I was going to attack him. The referee was in the way.'

Joshua grazed the referee's face with a left hook and John-Lewis wagged a finger at him briefly before letting the fight continue. 'I was worried for a moment or two that I might get disqualified,' Joshua said later.

Shortly after the fight resumed, Joshua walked Leo on to a left-right that made him stumble. The Italian tried to rally, tried to fight his way through the mental fog, but couldn't dent Joshua and found himself being drilled around the ring by thumping left-rights. Ringsiders got to their feet and screamed. The end of the fight looked to be only a clean punch or two away.

Joshua forced Leo to the ropes, landed a jab, slipped a countering jab and then smacked him on the jaw with a right hand that made his eyes roll. Joshua sensed he should go for the knockout and quickly jumped up through the gears, hammering the Italian with left-right after left-right until he crashed to the floor, a final scything right hand sending him semi-conscious to the canvas just as the referee moved in to stop the fight after just two minutes and 49 seconds of the opening round.

'It felt like the real deal,' said Joshua of professional boxing, 'two guys with their heart on their sleeve, trading.'

Hearn gushed afterwards, 'Big "Josh" is going all the way. This is just the start of a phenomenal journey.'

Earlier that day, in Moscow, there was a fight that showed where Joshua's journey might take him.

The top two heavyweights in the world had split a purse of $23m and Wladimir Klitschko had demonstrated there was a good-sized gulf between himself and his nearest rival, Alexander Povetkin, by winning a sometimes ugly fight unanimously on the judges' scorecards.

Joshua was asked how soon he might be fighting at that level.

'I'm not saying anything yet,' he answered.

Fight No 2
Paul Butlin

At: The Sheffield Arena

On: Saturday, 26 October 2013

Opponent's record: Fights 33 Wins 14 Losses 19

Joshua's weight: 16st 8.5lb

Opponent's weight: 16st 11.75lb

Scheduled for: 6 Rounds

Result: Joshua won by second-round stoppage

PAUL BUTLIN knew a boxing Joshua never will.

He squeezed in training himself around work and the school run and when it came to fighting, he either sold tickets to have winnable fights at home that earned him a few hundred pounds – or he took much harder fights away from home for much better money.

Mostly, he took hard fights for money – and lost.

From Oakham in Leicestershire, Butlin says he was 'fat and mouthy' in his teens and to keep the bullies at bay, he took up karate.

He won national honours and at 24, started boxing in the shed where Melton Amateur Boxing Club was based.

Twelve amateur bouts – six wins, six defeats – wasn't much of an apprenticeship, but 6ft 4in, 16st amateurs are hard to match and when Capitol Promotions said they would invest in him, Butlin decided to turn professional with them in 2002.

The Coventry promoters billed him as their 'Blonde Destroyer', got him a few wins, but then folded and the fights dried up.

To get fights, Butlin had to become an opponent. Not a journeyman.

'I've got a lot of respect for what journeymen do,' he said, 'but to me, a journeyman is someone who loses for money and I always had a go. I came to fight.'

He went across Europe fighting good-calibre opponents such as Johnathon Banks, Andrzej Wawrzyk, Johann Duhaupas and Edmund Gerber, often at short notice, and though he always lost, more often than not, Butlin heard the final bell. 'I got put down,' he said, 'but I got back up again.

'I always got treated really well when I went abroad. They put me up in nice hotels and the promoters seemed to like me. I knew how to sell a fight.

'When my opponents wanted to shake hands at the weigh-in, I stuck my head in their face. It helped sell the fight – and let everyone know I was there to fight, I was there to have a row. The promoters used to say to me, "You English are crazy."'

Pain wasn't an issue for Butlin, the tattoos that snaked their way from his ankle up to his neck were proof of that, and he was actually fond of laughing at his opponents after they had punched him very hard in the face.

The future Mrs Butlin didn't enjoy it as much, but though she asked him every day to retire from boxing, the hard fights gave him enough money and respect for him to keep going. Even in the company of the hardest of men, Butlin was respected.

'PAUL BUTLIN IS THE ONLY MAN OUT THERE!' boomed Tyson Fury after he had beaten John McDermott in June 2010, explaining that Butlin had stepped up to spar him when nobody else was answering the phone.

That respect wasn't always mutual.

As anyone who ever followed him on Facebook and Twitter knows, Butlin was always up for a social media spat.

He asked 'Sharon Briggs' for 'a straightener', told Jason Gavern where to go and whenever Dereck Chisora was mentioned, the pick-a-window snarl of the nightclub bouncer he was for years would spread across Butlin's face.

Following their second fight, at the York Hall in May 2009, Chisora was fined £2,500 and banned for four months for biting him.

'He said he did it because he got bored,' said Butlin, 'but he got bored because he couldn't knock me out.'

For that rematch, and many of his fights, Butlin trained himself at his own gym, Hard Knocks in Melton Mowbray.

The motto written on the gym wall was, 'Go hard or go home' and also on the wall was a huge photograph of Butlin celebrating his best win, a two-round knockout of Colin Kenna in the inaugural 'Prizefighter' in April 2008.

Kenna was around the domestic top ten at the time and Butlin hoped the victory might attract some backing.

But whenever the phone rang, it was only ever a matchmaker offering a tough fight and Butlin never could turn down a fight.

'I just asked what the money is,' he said, 'and as long as they didn't take the mickey, I said, "Yes."

'I always saw those fights as an opportunity and a challenge.

'If I won, it was massive and who else was going to go in there with them and have a go? I wasn't scared of any of them.

'I never cared who I fought. I was always in the gym and always healthy. I don't drink or smoke.

'I know they used me as a stepping stone, but I always came to fight. I was paid to have a go. I didn't lie down.'

Butlin had back-to-back losses going into the Joshua fight and their scheduled six-rounder at the O2 Arena was no way for a 37-year-old on a losing streak to turn his career around.

This was a fight Joshua was certain to win, but it would at least give him the chance to rate his power against others in the division.

Butlin had been punched on the nose by some top heavyweights and in his estimation, nobody hit him harder than Lucas Browne.

The limited Australian banger, a late convert to boxing after a divorce left him free to pursue his combat sport ambitions, blasted Butlin to the floor four times and stopped him in four rounds at the less-than-salubrious Oldham Sports Centre in April 2012.

Butlin found out how hard Joshua punched on a show at Sheffield Arena that was topped by welterweight contender Kell Brook facing Vyacheslav Senchenko, a former world champion best known for sending Ricky Hatton into retirement.

Butlin spoke beforehand of 'spoiling the party' and that motivated Joshua.

'He was saying certain things,' remembered Joshua. 'He was going to do this, he's going to spoil the AJ party. He got under my skin a little bit. No one is ruining the AJ party, it has just begun.

'I really wanted to put on another performance.

'Sheffield was my second home, I trained there as an amateur.'

For all Butlin's talk, staying on his feet for a couple of rounds would be considered a triumph.

He started the fight positively enough.

Butlin came out throwing jabs that mostly missed, then Joshua found the target with his jab.

'You don't realise how hard he hits,' said Butlin, 'until he hits you.

'He hit me with a jab and I thought, "Fuck!"'

The right hand carried even more weight and when it landed early in the second round, Butlin was flung to the floor in a heap, a gash on his left eyebrow that would later need nine stitches marking the point of impact.

'He pushed my jab out of the way,' he remembered, 'and bang! He hit me with a right hand over the top. It was such a fast shot, the best I've ever taken, but I still got up.'

Butlin was up at the count of five and, to the surprise of most, including Butlin himself, referee Howard Foster let the fight continue.

But whatever fight was left in Butlin was soon smashed out of him. Joshua attacked his ribs with a volley of heavy punches that had him looking hurt and disinterested and sensing that, his corner threw in the towel just as Foster stepped in between them to wave the fight off.

The three minutes and 50 seconds Butlin spent in the ring with Joshua made him rethink his list of heaviest punchers he had faced.

'He's just on another level,' he said. 'I took on [former domestic contender] Larry Olubamiwo with 24 hours' notice [losing in seven rounds], [former world-class cruiserweight and heavyweight] Johnathon Banks with three days' notice [losing in seven] and I had five days for the second Chisora fight [losing on points over eight].

'I had ten weeks for this one and he just destroyed me.

'I don't care who you are, if Joshua hits you on the chin, the fight's over.'

Fight No 3
Hrvoje Kisicek

At: The York Hall, Bethnal Green, London

On: Saturday, 14 November 2013

Opponent's record: Fights 11 Wins 5 Losses 6

Joshua's weight: 16st 5lb

Opponent's weight: 15st 9.5lb

Scheduled for: 6 Rounds

Result: Joshua won by second-round stoppage

'AFTER THAT, who's going to fight him?' asked a hugely impressed Paul Butlin.

'We will always be able to find opponents,' answered Hearn. 'It's just that we're going to have to pay them more money.'

Hrvoje Kisicek agreed to be Joshua's third professional opponent and the six-round fight provided the chance to compare his progress with another British heavyweight prospect.

Four weeks earlier, Kisicek, a 28-year-old from Croatia, had lasted the full six rounds with Hughie Fury in Whitwick, a former pit village in north-west Leicestershire.

Fury had turned professional at 18 years old after winning the World Junior Championships in Armenia and his father and trainer, Peter Fury, kept him busy.

He got him slots on televised shows when his stablemate and cousin Tyson Fury was boxing and Fury also learned his trade on small-hall bills, against tough journeymen like Kisicek.

That was Fury's 11th pro fight and he won it comfortably enough on points over six rounds, without ever having Kisicek in any sort of desperate trouble.

Kisicek went back home, got a win over a fighter with a record of nine fights and nine defeats, then returned to face Joshua on a show at the York Hall in Bethnal Green, east London.

Either he would take Joshua a few rounds – or Joshua would prove a point by beating him early.

Kisicek had some amateur pedigree having fought for Croatia in the 2003 European Junior Championship, but as a senior, the highlight was reaching the Croatian super-heavyweight final and his professional record was five wins plus six defeats.

The five wins came at the Joker's Gym in Split and there was every chance they were actually spars – or possibly not even that.

His handlers may well have just wanted to invent a good record for Kisicek so they could ship him abroad and start making money out of him.

These things happen in professional boxing.

The fact Kisicek had been capable enough to last six rounds with Fury gave the match with Joshua credibility, but there was only one possible outcome to the fight.

The fight was part of a 'Prizefighter' show that featured 47-year-old James 'Lights Out' Toney, a former world champion at three weights.

Toney, whose abrasive manner didn't make him too popular with either Sky Sports staff or his rivals, still had the classy moves and know-how of the quality fighter he had been, but didn't have the appetite for fighting anymore and lost a semi-final to Jason Gavern he could have easily won had he put a bit more into it.

Gavern went on to lose the final to Michael Sprott and watching it all was one of the best heavyweights of the previous three decades.

Larry Holmes, who succeeded Muhammad Ali as the world's dominant heavyweight and fought on until he was 52 years old, was in the United Kingdom on an after-dinner tour. He had a break in his schedule that allowed him to visit the York Hall and watch Joshua.

By the looks of things, he probably wasn't going to be watching Joshua for very long, however.

Kisicek didn't exactly ooze confidence during the masters of ceremonies' introductions. He looked fleshy and disinterested and when the fighters were brought together for the referee's instructions, it was obvious Joshua had every physical advantage imaginable.

This was a fight, ringsiders sensed, that would end when Joshua wanted it to end.

He answered the opening bell with a fast jab that brought gasps from the crowd and a response from Kisicek.

He rushed in crudely and Joshua took half a step back and clipped him on the top of his head with a left hook, a quality move. The punch stiffened Kisicek's legs briefly, but Joshua didn't show any interest in trying to end the fight there and then. He would say later he wanted to have some time in the ring to work on his jab, footwork and counter punching.

His jabs and counter punches soon raised a bruise around Kisicek's right eye and he came under fire in a neutral corner when Joshua unloaded a burst of fast punches.

Kisicek was able to escape and launched a rather clumsy left hook in the closing seconds of the round. Joshua saw the punch coming and it brushed harmlessly off his cheek, but he acknowledged the outclassed Kisicek's spirit with a tap of his glove at the bell. Kisicek was a fighting man, too.

Joshua decided this fight would end in the second round.

Early in the session, he had Kisicek hurt and holding, but again, he stood back, had a look and when he felt the time was right and the opening was there, he stepped in with a four-punch burst.

The first punch missed Kisicek's stomach – somehow – but the following left-right-left found his chin and dumped him on the floor. Nobody would have blamed the Croat had he decided to stay there, but at referee Marcus McDonnell's count of four he was on his feet and ready to carry on fighting.

Joshua knew the outclassed Kisicek was close to defeat and produced a classy finish. He stuck a hard jab in Kisicek's face and then dropped his hands by his sides, encouraging Kisicek to throw punches. It was a trap – and the Croat fell into it.

Joshua knew a countering lunge was coming and when it came, he comfortably swayed to safety and jumped all over the defenceless Kisicek, reeling off a rat-a-tat two-fisted burst of punches that knocked him into the ropes.

Joshua tried to ignore the referee's attempts to get between the fighters to stop the fight and Kisicek was happy to carry on trading punches, even though he was hopelessly outgunned and certain to be knocked off his feet at any moment.

At the second attempt, McDonnell dragged Joshua off Kisicek, to the Croat's disappointment. With a fighter's pride, he protested the stoppage was premature, but really, it was pointless letting the fight continue.

'I knew that guy had been in with some hopefuls and been the distance,' said Joshua when he looked back on the fight later in his career, 'so for me to get the stoppage showed where I was at.

'I felt I did it with ease as well.'

Upon leaving the ring, Holmes told Joshua, 'Do not rush, do not run before you can walk,' and he told dinner audiences that if Joshua kept progressing and didn't neglect his jab, he could be a dominant world heavyweight champion.

Fight No 4
Dorian Darch

At: The Motorpoint Arena, Cardiff

On: Saturday, 1 February 2014

Opponent's record: Fights 9 Wins 7 Losses 2

Joshua's weight: 17st 3.5lb

Opponent's weight: 17st 3lb

Scheduled for: 6 Rounds

Result: Joshua won by second-round stoppage

JOSHUA'S NEXT fight looked straightforward enough. Even his opponent thought so.

'I always try to win,' said 29-year-old Welshman Dorian Darch before the fight, 'but I'm a realist.

'I have got my limitations and I know I'm never going to be world champion.

'I also know Joshua is a huge guy and he's probably going to be too big for me.

'You never know, I could hit him on the button and my world could change, but I know there are levels in boxing.'

Defeats against Ian Lewison and Hughie Fury suggested Darch's level was short of British title class, but he didn't seem to mind too much.

He didn't take boxing too seriously.

'I earn decent money [as a civil engineer] and the boxing is pocket money for me,' he said once, 'and it keeps me off the beer.'

Darch might have run into Joshua sooner.

Joshua won the English ABA championship in 2011, a few weeks after Darch took the Welsh ABA title in only his 11th bout.

Had there been a Great Britain championship, as there had been the previous year, Darch and Joshua may have met.

But there was no Great Britain championship and for Darch, no point in continuing his amateur career either, though the boxer he beat in the Welsh final, Andrew Wyn Jones, went on to compete in the Commonwealth Games.

Darch watched Joshua at the London Olympics – 'I like watching the boxing with a couple of cans on a Saturday night,' he said – and thought him fortunate to beat both

Erislandy Savon in his opening contest and Roberto Cammarelle in the final.

By then, Darch was making his way in the professional ranks, under manager Steve 'Sammy' Sims, the former British featherweight champion.

Darch won his first six fights – and pleased the crowds. 'I just bore in,' he said. 'I will take one to land one.'

In his seventh fight, he took a few too many against Ian Lewison, a sometimes under-motivated talent from south London.

Darch suffered a broken jaw in his fourth-round defeat and though Hughie Fury didn't cause that sort of damage, he still won every round to inflict another loss.

Fury didn't sparkle and by matching Joshua with Darch, Hearn was again giving his fighter the chance to prove he was the better prospect.

Joshua had to wait to prove his point.

Twice the fight had to be rescheduled after Joshua pulled out, first with a bicep injury and then a trapped nerve in his shoulder.

When the fight eventually went ahead, Joshua conceded home advantage.

The Motorpoint Arena in Cardiff, where a featherweight match between up-and-coming Lee Selby and the faded Rendall Munroe topped the bill, was rather closer to Darch's Abderdare home than it was to Watford.

Every other advantage was with Joshua.

The record books state that at 6ft 2.5in, Darch is three and a half inches shorter than Joshua. Darch reckons it's more. 'He was huge,' he said. 'He's never three inches taller than me. I said to the officials, "You need a new fucking tape measure!" It was like standing in front of a big tree. I was thinking, "He's only a bit taller than me," but he was a lot bigger.'

Joshua reckoned Darch 'looked like a strong guy, he looked bullish. You know, that [Mike] Tyson build, short and stocky, quite heavy, so he looked like he could carry some weight behind his punches. So I knew I just wanted to get him out of there quick.

'I was watching Larry Holmes against Marvis Frazier [before the fight] and I saw the way Larry Holmes connected with a beautiful right hand.'

Holmes beat Frazier inside a round in 1983 and the chances were, the fight between Joshua and Darch would be over in similar time.

Darch was straight on the attack, trying the right hand and nearly landing it, but by the halfway stage of the opening round, it was getting hard for him as Joshua found the target with jabs that bloodied his nose.

Darch reckons he knows what he did wrong.

'I caught him clean with a right hand late in the first round,' he said, 'and that made him angry.

'Until then, I was doing okay. I could see his punches coming and I was slipping them. I wasn't winning the fight, but I was making him miss.'

Then Joshua didn't miss and whatever slim hopes Darch had of winning the fight vanished. 'My head was like a pinball after that,' he said.

There was a salvo of 15 unanswered punches from Joshua late in the opening round that had referee Terry O'Connor poised to step in. Darch started fighting back to dissuade him from stopping the fight, but looked groggy as he went back to his stool with his nose bloodied and a swelling under his right eye.

Early in the second, Joshua connected with a left-right that sent Darch wobbling backwards. He smiled, but was hurt. Darch slipped a right hand, but was defenceless when Joshua came back with a left hook that knocked him into the ropes.

This time, O'Connor decided he had seen enough.

'He hit me on the temple,' was how Darch explains the finish. 'I didn't really feel any pain, but my legs went and if the referee hadn't stopped it, he would have punched me through the ropes.

'My claim to fame is that he didn't drop me.

'I tried, but there are levels in boxing and I always knew I wasn't in Joshua's.

'I might have landed a punch that made the fight different, but he landed it.

'I had a go, picked up my five grand and went home.'

Fight No 5
Hector Avila

At: The Scottish Exhibition Centre, Glasgow

On: Saturday, 1 March 2014

Opponent's record: Fights 38 Wins 22 Losses 15 Draws 1

Joshua's weight: 17st

Opponent's weight: 16st 6lb

Scheduled for: 6 Rounds

Result: Joshua won by first-round knockout

JOSHUA HAD faced four fights, won them all by knockout, and it wasn't good enough.

The Darch bout had left him frustrated.

'With the amount of training I was going through, I should have performed better,' he said.

'You can't blame me for wanting to be perfect in a sport like boxing because all it takes is one mistake and I've got to start again.'

Joshua also said that at three minutes and 51 seconds the fight with Darch wasn't long enough for him to find his rhythm and really show what he can do.

He hoped his next opponent would stick around longer.

It seemed unlikely. Hector Avila was an Argentine known as 'El Tiburon', or 'The Shark', but at 38 years old and with 11 inside-the-distance defeats, including four inside the opening two rounds, he was looking rather toothless.

He didn't travel well either. Outside Argentina, his record was nine defeats from nine fights.

Avila did have a win going into the Joshua fight, over 43-year-old Marcelo Dominguez, a former WBC cruiserweight champion from the 1990s, and Hearn had another way of selling his six-round fight with Joshua.

British fans would remember – possibly – Avila lasting nine rounds with Dereck Chisora 11 months previously.

The interest here then was if it took Chisora nine rounds to stop Avila, how long would it take Joshua?

Chisora was also a product of Finchley and District Amateur Boxing Club and Joshua said that after he took up boxing, talk of Chisora's achievements inspired him.

Though he had won British, Commonwealth and European titles and fought for world honours, Chisora made a habit of fighting to the level of his opposition and against Avila, the north Londoner laboured, *Boxing News* describing a 'sluggish and largely uneventful contest. The fleshy Buenos Aires veteran lacked the ambition and skill to trouble Chisora.'

Chisora had an explanation for his sloppy performance.

The fight was the last of a long night's boxing at the Copper Box Arena and Chisora said he chose to take the fight into the later rounds out of spite. He wanted to keep the officials waiting to go home after they had kept him waiting to fight all night.

The fight with Avila would be the fifth of Joshua's career and given that Hearn had said he was building him in five-fight blocks, it was time to reassess.

'We did a sheet looking at my first five opponents,' said Joshua, 'and when you look at the guys Lennox [Lewis] and other Olympic gold medallists had [in their first five fights], I've had tougher fights.'

Tougher opponents maybe, but not tougher fights. Joshua was making short work of decent-looking opponents and giving crowds what they wanted to see.

Professional boxing, Joshua said, was 'about glitz and glamour. I'm there to entertain.'

The British public could be hard on their heavyweights. Frank Bruno and Lennox Lewis were booed when they plodded against inferior opposition early in their careers – and Joshua didn't want that. He had the public behind him and wanted to keep them on his side with clean, electrifying knockouts. Hearn felt that a good way to build a following for Joshua was to take him around the country for fights while he was on the way up.

Hearn knew that with his punch and personality, wherever Joshua went, he would make friends.

Even in Scotland, where Ricky Burns was defending his WBO lightweight title against Terence Crawford.

This was the night, Joshua would remember with a smile, when he became 'McJoshua'.

'People with Joshua's accent usually aren't that well received in Glasgow,' said Nick Halling, who commentated on the fight for Sky Sports.

'I was expecting he would get a lukewarm reception, at best. But once he made his appearance, the place erupted. It was like a rock star walking into a venue. Everywhere you looked, people were grinning in excitement and anticipation.

'He had the entire Glasgow crowd 100 per cent behind him. It was as though he was a returning hero.

'He has that impact on people – and it's not just because he is big. There's a warmth about him that's very natural. He has this thousand mega-watt grin and once people see it, they are eating out of his hand.

'Some people have a natural charisma – and Joshua is one of those people.'

Joshua came out of his changing room to the tribal thump of 'I'm Gonna Be (500 miles)', a Scottish drinking song if ever there was one, and on the way to the ring, he bumped every fist, returned every smile.

To the public, he was 'AJ' or 'Josh' in the same way Henry Cooper had been 'Our 'Enery' and Frank Bruno had been 'Big Frank'.

'I think being a boxer you have to be a man of the people,' said Joshua. 'It's old school, isn't it? When you think of boxing, you think of the Rocky films, you know what I mean?'

So long did it take Joshua to reach the ring, jokers at ringside wondered if by the time he got there, Avila would be flagging after four or five minutes' shadow boxing.

The Joshua mantra, 'Stay Hungry', was sewn into his gown, indicating that however much he achieved, it wasn't enough, while looking at Avila's waistline, he hadn't been hungry recently.

Avila was also short, the top of his head barely reaching Joshua's chin when referee Victor Loughlin brought them together for his instructions before the opening bell.

Avila tried to keep himself safe. He either circled the ring or burrowed in close. He wanted to be either too far away or too close to be hit. Joshua sized up what he had in front of him and then smacked Avila flush in the face with a hard double jab. Avila half blocked a following left hook, but appeared to feel the weight of the punch through his gloves and Joshua went for him, finding the gaps with body punches as the Argentine covered up desperately on the ropes.

Avila grabbed Joshua around the waist and after the referee separated them, he shot a glance at his corner. He looked panicky – and his next punch was an all-or-nothing shot.

Avila launched a big, slow right hand – and Joshua beat him to the punch with a short left hook. The blow caught Avila on his cheekbone and sent him tumbling over to the floor. He held his cheek while Loughlin counted over him, then got up at 'nine' and complained when the fight was waved off after only two minutes and 14 seconds of the first round.

Interviewers found Joshua more satisfied with his night's work this time.

'As the opponents get better, I want to keep doing that,' he said, and Hearn promised the opponents were going to get better. He also predicted that within six months, Joshua would be challenging for the British championship.

Fight No 6
Matt Legg

At: Wembley Stadium

On: Saturday, 31 May 2014

Opponent's record: Fights 9 Wins 7 Losses 2

Joshua's weight: 16st 12lb

Opponent's weight: 16st 3.5lb

Result: Joshua won by first-round knockout

CARL FROCH and George Groves were the perfect mismatch.

Froch was a proud veteran from Nottingham and Groves a too-clever-by-half young upstart from London who delighted in getting under his skin.

'He didn't give me any credit for what I'd achieved,' protested Froch and that, Groves would later say, was part of the game plan before he challenged Froch for his WBA and IBF super-middleweight titles in Manchester in November 2013. The idea was to wind up the prickly Froch and make him so desperate to put Groves in his place that he would 'run on to my right hand all night'.

In the first round, Froch ran into a Groves right hand and ended up on the floor. He picked himself up, fought his way back into the contest and though Groves led on all three judges' scorecards after eight rounds, he looked to be fading.

Froch was still strong and with Groves wobbly and tiring in the ninth, but not desperately hurt, referee Howard Foster jumped in to stop the fight.

Outrage followed.

Groves felt he had been the victim of an injustice, the public had been robbed of seeing the rivalry through to its conclusion and Foster became the target of the public's fury.

Eddie Hearn did what any promoter would do. He tried to set up a rematch. He sent out a tweet on social media site Twitter asking who wanted to see it – and within 24 hours, he had 37,000 replies.

Against his father's advice, Hearn booked Wembley Stadium for the fight and within an hour of tickets going on sale, 60,000 were sold.

The remaining 20,000 were soon snapped up.

'That's why I went with Matchroom,' Joshua told Sky Sports, 'for the shows they are producing.

'[For me] it's about dealing with the crowd, the expectation – and my opponent ain't got nothing to lose.

'This is the stage for him to relight his career.'

Matt Legg always was up for a fight. Even when he had three or four opponents at the same time.

Legg was a 36-year-old ex-prizefighter when he went out in his home city, Milton Keynes, on New Year's Eve, 2012.

That night, he was targeted by a gang and Legg being Legg, he took them on. He was handling himself well enough until he became short of breath and, disappointed with his lack of fitness, he decided he had to get back in the gym, get in shape and then ask his attackers for what he would call 'a straightener'.

Legg posted footage of a training session on social media and manager Mervyn Turner got in touch and suggested a comeback.

Legg liked the idea and when he made his return, at a Milton Keynes nightclub called Wonderworld Xscape on a Sunday afternoon, there weren't any empty seats.

Not all of Legg's supporters could get to his fights.

Michael Peterson never made it.

Better known as Charles Bronson, labelled 'Britain's most notorious criminal' by the tabloid press for his violent, erratic behaviour, he had been writing to Legg for several years after a cousin who lived in Milton Keynes put them in touch.

Bronson would wish Legg luck in his fights, moan about reality television stars, and Legg campaigned for his release.

Joshua did get to Legg's fights.

'I talked to him at the weigh-in before we fought,' remembered Legg, 'and he said, "I remember you. I used to support you."

'He was there when I made my comeback at Watford Town Hall.'

That was in 2008.

Legg had turned professional with Frank Maloney in 2001 after reaching the ABA super-heavyweight final.

He won his first three fights, then ran into Alvin 'Slick' Miller's right hand and drifted away.

Legg returned to boxing six years later and chalked up a couple more wins before knee surgery ruled him out for a further five years. Again, he came back, at 38 years old, with the intention of shedding the rust as quickly as possible, then taking some risks.

'Prizefighter' was just what he had in mind.

Legg described the eight-man tournament as 'a short cut'. That is, he could move his career forward several steps in one night, and the quarter-final draw for the international heavyweight 'Prizefighter' at the York Hall in November 2013 offered him rather more than that.

Joshua had his third professional fight on the show, against Hrvoje Kisicek, but if Legg beat James 'Lights Out' Toney over three rounds, he would steal a few headlines from him.

Now a 47-year-old veteran of 88 fights, in his prime, Toney had the talent to back up his boasts. He won world titles at middleweight, super-middleweight and cruiserweight and had fought Michael Nunn, Roy Jones Jnr, Mike McCallum, Evander Holyfield and more.

Legg, considered a win or two away from a Southern Area title fight at the time, described the draw as 'a dream come true' and going into the last round, he was still very much in the contest.

With the fight in the balance, Toney woke up and buzzed Legg with a right-hand counter, described as 'the best punch in boxing' by its recipient, which led to the stoppage.

Legg got back in the ring and hoped to get a shot at the Southern Area championship. Then he got the call to fight Joshua.

'I was working on a building site carrying plastering boards up and down ladders all day long,' said Legg, 'so I was super fit.

'I was told they were struggling to find an opponent for Joshua, but I said "Yes" straightaway. I was really up for it.

'I trained to fight all out for two rounds and after that, I just had to take what was coming.'

The game plan was, had to be, to get close to Joshua and unload and, for a moment or two, Joshua looked a bit unsettled as Legg set about him.

'The ring was tiny,' said Joshua, 'and before I knew it he was in my corner swinging hooks.'

There was a swinging left hook from Legg that whistled just past Joshua's chin, bringing gasps from ringsiders. 'I put everything into that shot,' said Legg, 'and if I had caught him, who knows what would have happened?'

Joshua threw a flurry of punches to escape the corner, got back to the centre of the ring and spotted an opening.

'The moment I stopped moving my head,' said Legg, 'he hit me.'

The punch Joshua hit him with was a pulverising short right uppercut – and it dropped Legg.

'I tried to get up,' he said, 'but I couldn't see anything.

'It felt like there was blood pouring out of my eyes.'

The punch had fractured Legg's eye socket, but despite his blindness and excruciating pain, he still almost beat the count. Referee Steve Gray reached the count of ten just as Legg pulled himself upright. The time was one minute and 23 seconds of the opening round, Joshua's quickest win so far.

'I had three months of nerve damage in the side of my face,' said Legg. 'For two months I had no feeling. It was numb.'

Hearn predicted that within three years, Joshua would be topping the bill at Wembley Stadium and later that night, Froch's right-hand thunderbolt in the eighth round brought an emphatic full stop to his rivalry with Groves.

Fight No 7
Matt Skelton

At: The Echo Arena, Liverpool

On: Saturday, 12 July 2014

Opponent's record: Fights 36 Wins 28 Losses 8

Joshua's weight: 17st 1lb

Oppontent's weight: 17st 1lb

Scheduled for: 6 Rounds

Result: Joshua won by second-round stoppage

A FUNNY thing happened to Matt Skelton in the gym a while ago.

'I was hitting the bags and this instructor was watching and didn't look impressed,' said Skelton.

'I told him, "I did have a few pro fights."'

Skelton did more than that. He won a Lonsdale belt outright, challenged for world honours and at the ripe old age of 49, he fancied his chances of bashing Joshua.

The names of Joshua's first six opponents, Emanuele Leo, Paul Butlin, Hrvoje Kisicek, Dorian Darch, Hector Alfredo Avila and Matt Legg, were unrecognisable except to those in the trade and hardcore boxing fans.

Skelton was rather better known.

Turning professional at 34 after successful careers in kickboxing and K1, he won the British title within 19 months of his debut, a record, added Commonwealth and European titles and went into the record books as the oldest first-time challenger for the world heavyweight championship.

Skelton was a week shy of his 41st birthday when he lost on points to southpaw Ruslan Chagaev for the WBA title in January 2008.

Known as 'The Bedford Bear', Skelton never made any pretence of being anything other than what he was. 'I'm never going to dance like Muhammad Ali,' he told me once, but with his granite chin, huge heart and impressive fitness, he would slug with anyone.

Now 49 years old, the oldest active pro in Britain at the time, Skelton had been out of the ring for 16 months, since a points loss to John McDermott that was proof of his decline.

Seven years earlier, Skelton had blasted out McDermott in only 79 seconds in a British title defence.

'I didn't make any official announcement [about his retirement],' said Skelton, 'but my mind was made up. The hunger wasn't there anymore.'

The appetite returned when a fight with Joshua was mooted.

Skelton didn't need the money. He had earned well from fighting in K1 and invested wisely. 'I earned a good living out in Japan, invested in properties and by the time I turned pro, I was fairly financially secure,' he said.

Money wasn't Skelton's motivation.

'As old as I am and as silly as it sounds,' he said at the time, 'I enjoy a good fight.'

This didn't look like a good fight for Skelton to take. Joshua was a fighter on the way up, Skelton a fighter on the way down.

These matches are commonplace in professional boxing, of course, when a prospect looks to get a good name on their record and the question here wasn't whether Joshua would beat the old and rusty Skelton, but rather, how good he would look beating him.

Skelton was known for his resilience and though stopped by Kubrat Pulev and David Price before, both times he was unravelled by body shots and the intrigue for Joshua watchers was whether he could knock the veteran off his feet him with a blast to the chin.

Skelton reckoned he was too hard for that.

As a boy he had played football for Bedford Schools, but gave it up for rugby because he preferred all the pushing and shoving. He gave up rugby after discovering kickboxing.

Skelton won a world kickboxing title and gained credibility by fighting on the tough K1 circuit in Japan where fighters use knees and elbows, as well as fists and feet.

'The British Steamroller', as he was known, went back and forth to Japan 'for about four and a half years' and it wasn't uncommon for him to be asked for his autograph.

Unhappy with a K1 defeat, Skelton decided to improve his hands and was pointed to Kevin Sanders.

Best known for training Nigel Benn, Sanders liked the look of Skelton and tried to talk him into boxing.

Skelton thought he was too old, but after he sparred Mathew Ellis, then around the domestic top ten, the advice was the same.

Skelton should turn professional.

He did turn professional, sent his debut opponent to hospital and walloped his way up the rankings.

Skelton took the British title off Michael Sprott, just 19 months after his debut, and captured the Lonsdale belt to keep with wins over Keith Long, Mark Krence and McDermott.

He reversed a loss to Danny Williams, repeated his win over Sprott and eight days before his 41st birthday, got a shot at the world title.

Skelton came up short against Chagaev, losing unanimously on the scorecards, but won the European title in his next fight and stayed in domestic contention.

Throughout his career, reporters found Skelton to be a good natured-interviewee,. He told me once his ambition was to appear in soap opera *EastEnders*, but was in mischievous mood at a press conference before the Joshua fight.

He wondered aloud whether Joshua would turn out to have the same flaws as Audley Harrison.

Harrison and Joshua looked as different as it was possible to look early in their careers.

Harrison was a cautious southpaw who struggled to get journeymen under control, while Joshua was walking through whoever was put in front of him on the way up.

For the first time in his pro career, Joshua went into a fight without Tony Sims in his corner. 'It was a holiday I'd promised my wife,' he explained later. 'It was our first holiday in 25 years on our own, without the children. It was a bit of a hard one to get out of.'

In his absence, brother Peter Sims took over and along with everyone else who had any knowledge of British boxing, he knew what to expect from Skelton.

At the opening bell, he stuck his head down, marched forward and let fly with right hands.

'I was rough and ready,' said Skelton, 'and I liked to dominate, but he stood his ground. He could mix it. He could get down and dirty, which I wasn't expecting.'

Referee Steve Gray told them both to clean up their work at one point and when Joshua mauled Skelton, ringsiders sought shelter as the ropes above them sighed under the strain.

Point proved, Joshua got back to the centre of the ring and smiled as he jabbed, feinted and probed for openings.

He liked a fight as well.

Skelton burst out laughing after Joshua connected with a right hand, but the news that Joshua had found his range with his biggest punch was nothing for him to be pleased about and the bell came at a good time for him.

Early in the second, Joshua again showed he could match Skelton when they mauled on the inside and then started to push him back with jabs.

Joshua manoeuvred Skelton towards the ropes and landed a clobbering right hand high on his head that dazed him and sent him stumbling into the path of another right hand that had everything behind it. Skelton was in desperate trouble and one more right-hand piledriver propelled him into the ropes – and down. He lay on his front until the count of around seven and hauled himself up at nine.

Skelton had to get through 35 seconds until the bell – and couldn't. Joshua sent him reeling back into a neutral corner with his next attack and the referee jumped in.

Grounded as ever, Joshua afterwards said he would have rather fought Skelton when he was at his peak several years earlier.

'His power didn't make me go, "Wow!" and I didn't come out of the ring in a lot of pain,' remembered Skelton, 'but he was quick and accurate.

'When Joshua hit me, I didn't think, "Wow, that was a good shot," I didn't have time to think anything. I didn't see the punches coming and the next thing I knew I was on the floor.

'The punches were quick, sharp and clean. He didn't waste anything.'

Fight No 8
Konstantin Airich

At: The Manchester Arena

On: Saturday, 13 September 2014

Opponent's record: Fights 32 Wins 21 Losses 9 Draws 2

Joshua's weight: 17st 2.5lb

Opponent's weight: 16st 1.25lb

Scheduled for: 8 Rounds

Result: Joshua won by third-round stoppage

JOSHUA WAS going to have his eighth professional fight in Dublin on 30 August.

But after bill-topper Matthew Macklin was injured, the show was cancelled and Joshua instead headed to Austria, where Wladimir Klitschko was training for his 26th world heavyweight title fight, against Kubrat Pulev.

Klitschko was always looking for sparring partners. He wanted to stay sharp and motivated – and knew it was important to keep an eye on the competition.

He remembered his late trainer, Emanuel Steward, telling him, 'Look at the sparring partners and don't forget that some are going to end up as your opponents.'

Klitschko sparred around 20 rounds with Joshua – and was impressed.

'I think Joshua has the greatest potential I have ever seen in another heavyweight,' he said.

'Being the Olympic champion says he has the technique and he also has strength and the desire to learn.

'I had Olympic champions and former world champions in my camp, but his attitude was totally different.

'He was not trying to impress anybody. He backed off, he was sitting on the side, not talking too much. He was watching, learning, asking questions. He was very polite. He was different to the others.

'He didn't see everything back then, but he got to know where I train, how I train, the rules. He got the vibe.'

Joshua said, 'What I learned from him is keep your head down and put in the work and show what you're about in the ring. That's what I'm trying to do.'

He learned more than that. Klitschko gave Joshua some technical advice, telling him to sit back a bit more when he throws his punches. It was advice Joshua took on board.

The way Joshua dealt with Skelton convinced Hearn to step him up to eight rounds and increase the level of his opposition.

His next two fights would be against Konstantin Airich and should all go well against him, four weeks later, Joshua would fight Denis Bakhtov, for the vacant WBC International belt.

There was also talk that should all go well against Airich and Bakhtov, Joshua would make a move towards the British title by fighting veteran Michael Sprott.

But first, Airich.

Earlier in his career, it seemed Airich, born in Kazakhstan and based in Germany, had the potential to be a European champion.

He had a good amateur grounding, a reported 99 bouts, before turning professional in 2007, but by the time he faced Joshua, he was 35 years old and it had become clear he was never going to reach European level.

Airich lacked the size and power to break through, but was considered a decent enough stepping stone who always came to fight and sometimes lost early.

On a previous trip to Britain, the towering Tye Fields, a 6ft 8in American southpaw with heavy hands, put him away in 74 seconds during a 'Prizefighter' for international heavyweights, and Manuel Charr whacked him out in only 44 seconds.

On better nights, Airich reversed a points loss to capable Ondrej Pala with a stoppage and up a level or two, he went the distance with skilled-but-lazy Cuban Odlanier Solis and

Vyacheslav Glaskov, both of whom challenged for world honours.

This looked a decent match, the step up Joshua needed, but once they met at the weigh-in, it was clear that, physically, it was a mismatch.

Airich was a short and stumpy 6ft 1in, Joshua an imposing, muscular 6ft 6in.

If he was going to have any sort of chance, Airich had to get close – and Joshua didn't let him. He kept Airich where he could hit him – and Airich couldn't hit him back.

Airich knew his job and was able to keep his chin out of harm's way and even dug in left hooks to the body after slipping Joshua's jab. They had no effect, other than to stir Joshua into retaliation. He blasted back with left-rights that, though blocked by Airich's gloves, still knocked him back and confirmed Joshua was in charge.

Joshua took his time, seeing what punches worked, keeping Airich guessing and rectifying mistakes here and there.

Airich spotted a gap in Joshua's defences in the second and launched a looping right hand.

The punch didn't trouble Joshua, it landed harmlessly on his cheek, but he smiled in acknowledgement of his error and raised his left glove an inch or two.

He then got back behind his thumping, disheartening jab and put together a fast three-punch combination that knocked Airich's gum shield out of his mouth in the final minute of the round.

The break to replace the gum shield meant a reprieve for Airich, but Joshua, and everyone else watching, knew it was only a matter of time before he got the knockout.

He didn't mind waiting until the third round – for the first time in his professional career.

Early in the round, Joshua landed the punch that convinced him to go through the gears. He dazed Airich with a right hand and then punched him to the ropes and pounded him to the floor. He added one more punch when Airich was on one knee to earn a warning from referee Steve Gray.

Airich dragged himself off his knees, on to his feet and straight back into trouble.

He had the pride to carry on, but was never going to be able to keep Joshua off him.

Joshua didn't give him a chance to escape the ropes, pumping out hard punches from both hands and after a left hand knocked back Airich's head, the referee decided he had seen enough and waved the fight off after one minute and 16 seconds of the round.

Fight No 9
Denis Bakhtov

At: The O2 Arena, Greenwich, London

On: Saturday, 11 October 2014

Opponent's record: Fights 49 Wins 38 Losses 9

Joshua's weight: 16st 12.5lb

Opponent's weight: 16st 4lb

Scheduled for: 12 Rounds

Vacant WBC International heavyweight title

Result: Joshua won by second-round stoppage

JOSHUA HAD thrashed his first eight opponents inside three rounds apiece and the story from the gym was, his sparring partners were also struggling to take his power.

Sims said that even with the added protection of bigger gloves and head guards, Joshua's sparring partners were unable to last four rounds with him.

Perhaps Denis Bakhtov could give him a few much-needed rounds?

'Joshua's biggest test,' read the *Boxing News* headline ahead of his ninth fight. 'Can Bakhtov take him rounds or even defeat the Olympic hero?'

The Russian had previously burst the bubble of a fighter who once claimed he would be 'the best heavyweight to ever come out of Britain'.

Blackpool playboy Mathew Ellis fell way short of that. He was exposed by Bakhtov, who stopped him in five to keep the WBC International title.

But that was more than a decade ago and by the time he faced Joshua, Bakhtov was a 35-year-old, 49-fight veteran known as a tough opponent on the European circuit.

The WBC International title he had defended against Ellis didn't prove to be a stepping stone to a shot at world honours, the way it subsequently did for Wladimir Klitschko and Bermane Stiverne.

Points losses to contenders Sinan Samil Sam, Juan Carlos Gomez, Vyacheslav Glaskov, Alexander Ustinov and Andrzej Wawrzyk put paid to any world title ambitions Bakhtov may have once had.

The record showed Bakhtov, a hard veteran with a hard veteran's face, wasn't in the habit of turning fights down, but he apparently took some convincing to fight Joshua.

Initially, Bakhtov turned the fight down and then had a rethink, presumably after being offered more money.

He would be a good scalp for Joshua and if he could force the stoppage, that would make a statement.

Bakhtov hadn't been stopped since 2005, but there had been signs of vulnerability during a points win over Airich only three months earlier and every possible advantage was with Joshua.

He was a decade younger, six and a half inches taller and clearly the bigger puncher.

Boxing News predicted a win for Joshua in around five rounds and there were signs in the opening seconds that Bakhtov may be the fighter to take him a few rounds.

He swerved his upper body this way and that to make Joshua miss with jabs, but then the Englishman landed a right hand, slicing open a cut on the corner of Bakhtov's left eyebrow. The sight of blood put a smile on Joshua's lips. He felt that punch had got Bakhtov under control.

Joshua looked comfortable, comfortable enough to smile when his feints didn't prise open Bakhtov's defences, but never too comfortable. He got his hands up when Bakhtov steamed into him.

Bakhtov launched an attack in the final minute of the opening round, Joshua gave ground and with perfect timing let go a short right hand that landed flush on Bakhtov's chin and sent a shiver down his legs.

Joshua stuck his tongue out as the Russian staggered back a few steps and Bakhtov shrugged in acceptance. He had been nailed by a terrific punch.

The next two right hands Joshua tried were blocked, but he kept the big punches coming. Mostly, they hit arms and gloves as Bakhtov tightened his defences and, sensing the knockout wasn't going to come, Joshua called off his attack. Moments later, the bell went.

Bakhtov came out for the second round throwing punches and leaving gaps.

Joshua found the gap for a chopping right hand to the chin that had Bakhtov backing up to the ropes.

Joshua went after him. Bakhtov tried to fight his way out of trouble, but Joshua brushed off the punches and set about beating him up with hooks and uppercuts.

The crowd screamed as Bahktov stumbled to the adjacent ropes.

Bakhtov kept his hands up, but with Joshua putting everything into every punch, he was still feeling the force of the blows through his gloves and he wasn't punching back.

Referee Ian John-Lewis appeared set to intervene, had second thoughts and then did jump in after a left-right-left sent Bakhtov crashing into the ropes.

The ending didn't satisfy Joshua, who revealed a malicious, Mike Tysonesque streak when interviewed by the press afterwards.

'I don't like it when they step in and stop the fight,' said Joshua. 'I want them to be on the floor, cold.

'I could see that I was hurting him and it's fun. He would do the same thing to me. If he had me up against the ropes punching my head in, he would love it.'

The stoppage was still a notable result, but as ever, Joshua stayed grounded, grading his performance at only one out of ten.

'Why? Because I was supposed to beat Denis Bakhtov,' he explained.

'He's not supposed to beat me.'

Joshua added, before heading back to his changing room for 30 minutes of pad work, 'I've got the potential.

'But that's all it is. It's not the reality.'

Hearn was rather more excitable, saying Joshua is 'going to clear out the heavyweight division' and adding, 'Joshua will be filling Wembley Stadium one day.

'He's the ultimate crossover star. A lot of that's to do with his success at the Olympics, his exposure on BBC One, and the fact that he's humble and he looks like a superhero. He's got it all.'

Fight No 10
Michael Sprott

At: The Echo Arena, Liverpool

On: Saturday, 22 November 2014

Opponent's record: Fights 64 Wins 42 Losses 22

Joshua's weight: 17st 2lb

Sprott's weight: 17st 5lb

Scheduled for: 10 Rounds

Eliminator for the British heavyweight championship

Result: Joshua won by first-round stoppage

JOSHUA'S FIGHTS seemed to be taking a similar pattern.

'In the first round, they come out, they move their head, they slip the first jab, they slip the second jab, but then I'm starting to hit them with my jab,' he told *Boxing Monthly*.

'In the second round, they either get hit too many times early on or they hold until the bell and then get stopped in the third round.

'The first round is the warm-up, the second round is the punishment and the third round is the finish.

'I want more. I look forward to the days when I'm tested.'

The subject of who would give Joshua that test was much discussed by fans and pundits.

The consensus was that it probably wouldn't be Michael Sprott.

Matching Joshua was a difficult job.

That he had won his first nine professional fights in a combined total of 35 minutes and 13 seconds suggested stiffer opponents were needed, but as good as Joshua was looking, Hearn didn't want him to jump up too far, too soon.

Boxing News came up with a list of possible opponents topped by Kevin Johnson, a skilled but negative American guaranteed to take him a few rounds, while, looking further ahead, Hearn said David Price and even David Haye could face Joshua in the next 12 months.

Provided, as seemed a near certainty, he got past Sprott.

The 39-year-old from Reading was a well-respected veteran with a long, hard career behind him. He turned pro in 1996 after reaching the ABA super-heavyweight final – 14 years before Joshua won the title – and had eight fights at British, Commonwealth and European championship level.

He shared a pair of dramatic fights with Audley Harrison, lost two of three fights with Danny Williams, there were disputed losses in Europe and even when he won, doors didn't open for Sprott the way they might.

Sprott also sparred many rounds with the Klitschko brothers, Wladimir and Vitali, and after 64 fights spread over 18 years, he was nearing the end.

Veteran manager and trainer Jim Evans had urged him to retire, but Sprott was determined to carry on and Evans decided that if Sprott was going to fight, it was better that he was there to keep an eye on him.

Sprott joined Evans in 2004 following the sudden death of trainer Johnny Bloomfield and trained in the gym Evans had built in the garden of his bungalow in Maidenhead.

'I sparred them all in there,' said Sprott. 'David Haye, Audley Harrison, Dereck Chisora.'

Evans was there with Sprott when he won the International Heavyweights 'Prizefighter' at the York Hall in November 2014.

Joshua had his third pro fight on the same bill, stopping Hrvoje Kisicek inside a couple of rounds, and wins over Damian Wills, Brian Minto and Jason Gavern convinced Sprott he could still compete at a decent level and make money.

The British Boxing Board of Control justified the Joshua–Sprott match by making it an eliminator for the British championship.

That was fair given Sprott's credentials and the way Joshua had been knocking his opponents out, but still, nobody in the trade really wanted to see the fight. There were genuine fears for Sprott's health. The best that could be hoped for was a quick Joshua win, with Sprott not taking too much punishment.

The Times reckoned Sprott was ten years past his best, and even in his prime, Evans had found him an infuriating talent. 'I never know which Michael is going to turn up,' he said once. 'He can play with the Klitschkos one day and lose to a novice the next.'

Whatever Sprott turned up to face Joshua, he looked to be in trouble. 'I know I'm in for a hard time,' admitted Sprott. 'He's hungry, a big puncher and he's 25.'

Even Sprott, it seemed, was struggling to convince himself he had a chance of winning the fight.

Sprott said his inspiration was Nigel Benn's tragic, back-from-the-brink win over Gerald McClellan a couple of decades previously.

Benn absorbed a vicious pummelling from McClellan in the early rounds, then rallied to stop him in ten rounds, inflicting life-changing injuries.

'I was going to find my way through the first few rounds and then take it from there,' said Sprott of his game plan.

Joshua was respectful, talking about Sprott's experience and his own growing fame.

'I haven't had this success from 12 years old and always known this was going to happen,' he said.

'I've had a bit of bad and a bit of good, so I am not going to get carried away because I want to keep this going and I have to keep my head on my shoulders.'

The show at Liverpool's Echo Arena was topped by feuding cruiserweights Tony Bellew and Nathan Cleverly. Bellew did a good enough job of selling their rematch – Cleverly had beaten him on points to keep his WBO light-heavyweight title three years earlier – for Sky Sports to make the show pay-per-view.

Bellew won on points – cruiserweight suited him rather better than it suited Cleverly – and earlier in the evening, the crowd had seen Joshua demolish Sprott.

For the opening minute of the scheduled ten-round fight, the fighters jabbed and blocked and Sprott was as busy as Joshua.

He never fought just to get paid.

Joshua found there were openings when he went to the body, then aimed a left-right at Sprott's head.

Sprott appeared to half block the right hand with his gloves, but his legs trembled, signifying he was hurt, and Joshua went quickly through the gears.

He drove Sprott to the ropes with more left-rights and once he had him there, Joshua really unloaded.

He found the gaps in Sprott's guard with fast, heavy punches from both hands and referee Terry O'Connor jumped between them, maybe a punch or two later than some ringsiders would have liked.

The fight was all over after just 86 seconds and a stiff-legged Sprott was helped back to his corner by O'Connor and his cornermen.

Sprott would say the late Corrie Sanders hit him harder, but admitted, 'For a muscular man of that size, he had serious hand speed.'

Joshua shrugged afterwards, 'Now I've got to go to the changing room and do nine rounds of pads,' and gave his thoughts on his next opponent.

'He's a veteran,' said Joshua of Kevin Johnson. 'He knows how to stick around.'

Fight No 11
Jason Gavern

At: The Metro Radio Arena, Newcastle

On: Saturday, 4 April 2015

Opponent's record: Fights 51 Wins 26 Losses 19 Draws 4

Joshua's weight: 17st 7lb

Opponent's weight: 17st 6lb

Scheduled for: 8 Rounds

Result: Joshua won by third-round knockout

THE SCHEDULED fight with Kevin Johnson at the O2 Arena on 30 January had to be postponed after Joshua suffered a stress fracture in his back.

He said he felt the injury before fighting Michael Sprott, but went through with the fight anyway. Afterwards, he went to see a doctor and was told to take a break from fighting.

The time off gave Joshua time to think and he gave an insight into what he thought about in an interview before his 11th fight.

'Every day I think about failing,' he confessed in *Boxing Monthly*, 'not losing, because you can learn from a loss, but failing.

'The pressure to be great, saying I can be the next this or that, or saying I can't, is fuel to the fire.

'I want to be successful to thank those people that have helped me and backed me and to those that doubt me, I would want to say, "Think twice before you think your opinion is fact."

'Life in general is hard and there are people out there with real problems, so the pressure I feel is nothing.

'If it was about being content, I would give up now. I'm in a much better state than I was. It's about legacy and empire building for my kids and their kids.'

As for Jason Gavern, he just wanted to get his next fight out of the way.

At around a week's notice, he agreed to fight Joshua and wasn't convincing anyone he was going to mark the 50th bout of his professional career with a win.

'I've been in the ring with everybody – either in training or sparring or actually fighting – and I've got to say, Anthony

Joshua is one of the top three fighters I've ever been in with,' said the 36-year-old from Orlando, Florida, in an alarmingly frank interview after the fight was announced.

'Back in August last year, I was in camp with him for ten days. I guess we did 12 or 15 rounds together.

'Sparring with him sucked, I'm not going to lie to you. I was sore, my whole body hurt. Every time he hit me, it hurt and that was with bigger gloves on.

'Now I've got to fight him with smaller gloves on. Oh my God!'

Gavern had been around boxing long enough, he had turned pro back in 2003, to know what his role was. He knew Matchroom weren't looking for what he described as 'a Godzilla' to bring Joshua back against after his time out through injury.

They wanted someone like him – a reliable trial horse who would put up a show, preferably a reliable trial horse who would put up a show and had a profile in Britain.

British fans remembered Gavern as a likeable eccentric who reached a 'Prizefighter' final and let out a 'whoop' – or should that be 'wooo' – after he took a clean shot or sometimes, before he let his own hands go.

Gavern hadn't had a good result for a while, not since holding Johnathon Banks to a draw on a Wladimir Klitschko undercard four years earlier, and though still capable, he was taking fights at short notice for money and didn't talk like he was motivated to produce his best against Joshua.

Rather, he sounded scared.

He seemed to accept he had nothing to beat Joshua with and went into the fight with only one ambition – to last longer than anyone else had.

Gavern assured Hearn he would hear the bell for the fourth round.

Eight months earlier, he had lasted four rounds with Deontay Wilder, the unhinged American puncher who had gone on to win the WBC title.

Gavern retired on his stool after the fourth having been dropped twice.

Joshua played down the comparison with Wilder – he accepted the American was way ahead of him – and just concentrated on beating Gavern and regaining some lost momentum.

This was likely to be a rusty Joshua, the break of six months since the Sprott fight was the lengthiest of his career, and in Gavern, he faced a cagey veteran who could possibly spoil and make him think for a few rounds.

To get through the rounds, Gavern was told by his corner, 'Move, stay on the outside, get underneath his punches and get in close.'

Gavern also knew the importance of keeping away from Joshua's right hand.

To do that, he dipped to his right and Joshua readjusted, knocking Gavern on to his heels with left hooks in the opening round.

The only question was how long Gavern would be able to survive.

Joshua had him on the floor in the second, with a left-right combination. It wasn't the cleanest of knockdowns. Replays showed Joshua's right hand brushed Gavern behind the ear to put him on his knees and while referee Victor Loughlin counted over him, Gavern held his glove to the back of his head.

He got up at eight without any verbal protest and grabbed hold of Joshua around his waist.

Joshua shook him off and slammed a right hand off his jaw. His senses scrambled by the punch, Gavern again ducked low and tried to grab Joshua around the waist, but he couldn't get out of the way of a short, clubbing left hook and sank to his knees.

He was up at eight, shook his right fist to show he was ready to fight on and let out a 'wooo' of defiance after the bell sounded moments later with him fuzzy-headed again after shipping a left hook.

Joshua answered the bell for the third with a smile on his face. He had Gavern where he wanted him now he fancied, and landed a jab.

Gavern was soon grabbing again and then freed his arms and started punching on the inside. Joshua punched with him and his punches carried much more weight. Gavern went sliding to his knees in a corner. Even when Gavern was on the floor, Joshua struggled to free himself from his grip. He was still grabbing at his feet.

Still proud and determined to keep his promise to Hearn, Gavern got up again – for a third time – and when the fight restarted, he slung a huge right hand in desperation.

Joshua saw the punch coming and dodged it with a smile, took a couple of body punches after Gavern bulled his way in close and then got his left hand working again and put together a left-right-left combination.

Gavern slipped the left and right, but ducked into the final, short left hook and ended up flat on his back.

He started his rise at the count of six, grabbed on to the ropes and was trying to decide whether it was worth getting up or not when referee Victor Loughlin made the decision for him.

He waved the fight over at the count of eight.

Joshua went to help Gavern to his feet, Gavern asked for a bit longer to recover – and both fighters laughed.

'Joshua's the future of the heavyweight division,' Gavern told reporters afterwards.

He explained later, 'A big guy like him shouldn't move as well as he does. He moves so fast, especially on the inside. He threw a triple hook on the inside with me and I didn't even know where it came from. It's crazy how fast his punches are.'

Fight No 12
Raphael Zumbano Love

At: The Barclaycard Arena, Birmingham

On: Saturday, 9 May 2015

Opponent's record: Fights 49 Wins 36 Losses 10 Draws 1

Joshua's weight: 17st 10lb

Opponent's weight: 16st 12lb

Scheduled for: 8 Rounds

Result: Joshua won by second-round stoppage

START OF THE JOURNEY . . . referee Ian John-Lewis indicates Emanuele Leo can take no more and Joshua's professional career is underway with a first-round win

THE HARDER THEY COME . . . heavyweight hardman Paul Butlin ships a right hand. Butlin would say that in 41 fights, nobody hit him harder

TAKE THAT . . . Joshua blasts veteran Matt Skelton on his way to win No 7

MAKING A STATEMENT . . . Denis Bakhtov was expected to give Joshua a test in his ninth fight. He didn't.

OVER AND OUT . . . Joshua sends Raphael Zumbano Love crashing with a right hand

WHO SAYS KEVIN JOHNSON CAN'T BE KNOCKED OUT ? . . . Joshua proves a point in fight No 13

NO LOVE LOST . . . Joshua and Dillian Whyte continue trading punches at the end of the first round of their grudge fight. Referee Howard Foster is trying to keep them apart.

THE END OF THE ARGUMENT . . . Joshua knocks out Dillian Whyte

ON HIS WAY TO THE TITLE . . . Joshua has the soon-to-be-former IBF heavyweight champion Charles Martin heading to the canvas

AND THE NEW . . . the celebrations begin after Joshua wins the IBF title in only his 16th professional fight

STILL THE CHAMP . . . Joshua has Dominic Breazeale close to defeat in his first defence of the IBF title

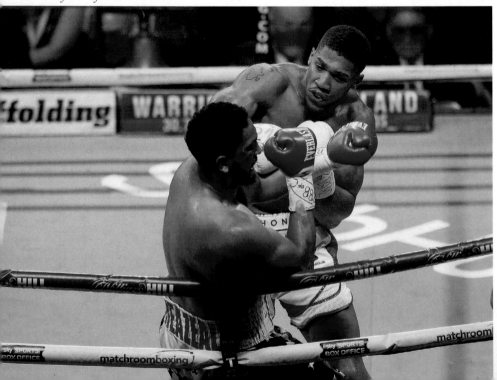

HE THINKS IT'S ALL OVER . . . but there was still plenty of fight left in Wladimir Klitschko after this fifth-round knockdown

WHAT A PUNCH . . . Wladimir Klitschko feels the force of Joshua's right uppercut in the 11th round and their 'Fight of the Century' will soon be over

WHAT A CHIN…
Carlos Takam was a
stubborn challenger for
Joshua's belts

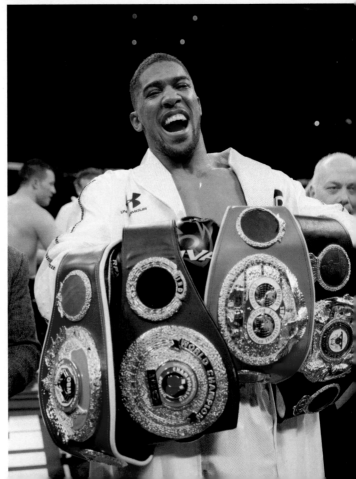

WHAT A CHAMP…
Anthony Joshua poses
with his belts after his
WBA, IBF, WBO and
IBO Heavyweight
Championship
title fight against
Joseph Parker at the
Principality Stadium
on 31 March, 2018 in
Cardiff, Wales

SOMEONE WHO could see the future reckoned there could be some trouble ahead for Joshua.

'Mickey Francois' made that prediction.

'Francois' would read palms and tarot cards and when he looked into Joshua's future, he saw a bit of bother for him at the Barclaycard Arena in Birmingham.

'Without a doubt,' he said, 'this is the toughest opponent Joshua has faced so far.'

'Francois' was also known as Mickey Helliet, a bilingual law graduate with a stable of 70 fighters he kept busy.

Helliet staged regular small-hall shows and was forever wheeling and dealing from his Chelsea flat to get fights for his journeymen, including Raphael Zumbano Love.

He was a 34-year-old from Brazil and just the sort of opponent Joshua and his team wanted to see him against in his 12th professional fight.

Mostly, Joshua had been fighting shorter opponents who looked to tuck up tight defensively and then throw counter punches.

The feeling was that Love had the requisite height, standing at 6ft 4in, and ambition, with a record of 36-10-1, to pose Joshua a different problem.

Love had 29 wins inside the distance, including nine in the first round, and could be expected to lead off and so test Joshua's defences and countering skills.

The likelihood is that whatever he did, Love would still get knocked out.

The list of top Brazilian heavyweights was a short one – Adilson Rodrigues had knocked about on the fringes of world class in the 1990s before finding his level when he faced George Foreman and Evander Holyfield – but

Helliet reckoned paid sparring with Bermane Stiverne had improved Love and he had boxing in his DNA.

His maternal grandfather, Ralph Zumbano, competed in the 1950 London Olympics, and Eder Jofre is a cousin.

Jofre is in the record books as Brazil's first world champion and is also regarded as possibly the country's best-ever fighter.

Love had never got anywhere near world level in his own professional career that he started in 2005 as Raphael Zumbano.

He became 'Raphael Zumbano Love' after a points win over Manuel Alberto Pucheta in November 2010.

The fight was held at the Companhia Athletica Brooklyn Gym in Sao Paulo, where Love trained, and the crowd included several of the gym's female members.

They celebrated with him after his hand was raised in victory and noticing this, someone shouted, 'This is Zumbano Love' – and that became his boxing name.

Love went into the Joshua fight as the Brazilian heavyweight champion and while that was only proof he was the best of a pretty average bunch, he had lasted into the tenth round with unbeaten American prospect Charles Martin and went the full 12 with 42-year-old Shannon Briggs, making him a measuring stick for Joshua.

'He can take a tremendous shot,' said Helliet of Love, 'and if you leave yourself open, he can get you out of there.

'Joshua could run into trouble if he steams into him and tries to finish it early.'

Love was taking the fight seriously, basing himself in London for around ten days before the fight, but still, this was another fight Joshua was expected to win with ease.

Hearn clearly thought so. He already had Joshua's next fight pencilled in, against Kevin Johnson three weeks later, and Johnson was ringside at the Barclaycard Arena, ready to sell the fight once Joshua had dealt with Love.

Tony Sims wasn't there. He was with Ricky Burns in America, where he was fighting Omar Figueroa, leaving his brother, Peter, in charge.

As Joshua's handlers had hoped, the Brazilian started positively behind his jab. But the jabs he aimed at Joshua were slow and they missed and there was a startled look on Love's face when Joshua connected with his jab.

Love would afterwards say he was shocked by Joshua's hand speed and how long his arms were. He would think he was at a safe distance and still get hit.

Once Love felt Joshua's jab, he had a rethink. He started circling the ring anxiously, occasionally wiping his fringe away from his eyes, and the crowd waited for the inevitable knockout.

It didn't come in the first round. Love got through it by not taking many chances.

At the end of the opening round, Max McCracken gave Joshua some good advice in his corner. 'Right hand over the jab,' said McCracken, the younger brother of Robert.

The Love jab, he had noticed, went out and came back slowly.

Joshua tried the right hand when Love jabbed at the start of the second round, but his timing wasn't quite there and he missed.

He got another chance moments later and this time, Joshua got everything right. He instinctively shot out a right hand that smacked Love flush on the chin and swept him off his feet. Love lay on his back until the count of four and by six, he got to his knees.

He stumbled and pulled himself back up again, regaining his feet just as referee Phil Edwards reached ten.

His legs then buckled again, sending him crashing into the ropes, as Joshua soaked up the crowd's applause following what commentators regarded as his most spectacular win yet.

The crowd's cheers turned to jeers after Kevin Johnson was introduced into the ring.

Dressed as always in sunglasses and chunky gold jewellery, Johnson looked Joshua up and down and said with a sneer, 'I got the antidote.'

The crowd booed louder.

Joshua said he looked forward to proving 'who the better man is' and the crowd cheered wildly.

Joshua went back to his hotel and rang Love. 'He wanted to know if everything was okay with me,' said the Brazilian, 'and to thank me for having fought.

'He said he respected me. He gained a fan.'

Fight No 13
Kevin Johnson

At: The O2 Arena, Greenwich, London

On: Saturday, 31 May 2015

Opponent's record: Fights 36 Wins 29 Losses 6 Draws 1

Joshua's weight: 17st 10.5lb

Opponent's weight: 17st 7lb

Scheduled for: 10 Rounds

WBC International heavyweight title

Result: Joshua won by second-round stoppage

TWO THINGS we knew about Kevin Johnson. One, he could talk a good fight and two, he gave everyone rounds.

Make that three things we knew. At some stage, Johnson was going to find himself fighting Joshua.

Joshua needed an opponent who could take him some rounds – and Johnson took everyone rounds.

The 35-year-old had fought Vitali Klitschko, Tyson Fury and Dereck Chisora in his 36-fight career – and he had taken them all the distance.

'It wasn't easy to hit him,' said Klitschko after outpointing Johnson in a defence of his WBC title in Switzerland in December 2009. 'He was always defensive.'

Johnson won just a single round on the three judges' scorecards that night and while he put his negative showing down to an injury to his left bicep, he was also very defensive against both Fury and Chisora. His cross-armed defence kept him safe and he only really let his hands go when he had to or thought he could pinch a win without getting hurt.

He didn't seem concerned about Joshua's punch.

'I'm going to fight with my hands down,' promised Johnson. 'He don't have no power.'

He also asked Hearn when the rematch would be after he had knocked Joshua out. Johnson wanted to know if it was worth going back to the States in between the fights.

Johnson was brought up by his mother, a church minister, and his grandmother in Atlanta, Georgia.

'I fought on the street all the time,' he remembered. 'I gave some lickings and I took some lickings.

'You would fight over your pride, your reputation, clothes, basketballs, bikes, anything you possessed. You'd fight over lunch money, even your girlfriend. That's why I caught 13 stitches in the back of my head.

'I was a good fighter in the streets and a lot of people knew about it so one guy decided to come behind me with a brick. He wanted what I had.

'That's the way it was, you gotta make sure when you hit someone you knock them out.

'I was a street guy so I never worried about working, it was survival of the fittest. You put a street guy on the street and he'll come back with money. You don't have to rob or steal nobody but you know what to do. You hustle. I was selling a bunch of things and I wasn't selling bikes and candy.'

Johnson was handed a five-year sentence after a street fight ended with his rival in a coma. He served two years and on his release, fought for the custody of his daughter Fatimah after her mother died in an accident, took up boxing and won 14 of 16 amateur bouts before turning professional in 2003.

The amateur career was a short one, but Johnson says he did a lot of learning in the gym and his teachers included Larry Holmes, who followed Muhammad Ali as the world's dominant heavyweight.

Johnson took from Holmes the importance of the jab and described himself as 'a very skilled and artistic boxer'.

Johnson did have ability and climbed into contention, but when he fought the division's best, he didn't show much ambition. He fought to get through the rounds rather than to win.

His durability and defensive skills meant Johnson was in demand as a sparring partner and he was in Bolton with the Furys, cousins Tyson and Hughie and trainer Peter, ahead of the Joshua fight.

Peter Fury, Tyson's uncle and Hughie's father, asked Clifton Mitchell to be in Johnson's corner when he fought Joshua.

'I told Peter, "I'm going to take all the credit when he wins,"' said Mitchell, who was the Furys' cuts man and had a good stable of fighters in his Derby gym.

Mitchell had once been a good heavyweight himself, good enough to fight for British and European honours, and guessed he wasn't going to be taking the credit for an upset win, even if there was a story – probably all it was – that Johnson placed a £1,000 wager on himself to win at lengthy odds.

Mitchell knew Johnson was there to stay safe – and get paid.

The question here wasn't whether Joshua would win, but what happened if he was taken beyond the opening few rounds, as seemed likely given Johnson's durability? Could Joshua slow the pace down or would he run out of steam? Could he do what nobody else had done and stop Johnson?

'If he [Joshua] goes ten rounds, it will be good for him,' said trainer Tony Sims, 'because he's gone nowhere near that and Johnson can take him that far.

'But if he stops him, we might see if he is the real deal.

'I personally think he [Joshua] will stop him.

'I don't think anyone can stand up to this fighter.'

Joshua wasn't making any bold predictions, only that it may take him a few rounds to figure Johnson out on a pay-per-view show that included his stablemates Kevin Mitchell and John Ryder.

Both returned to the changing room they shared with Joshua defeated, by Jorge Linares and Nick Blackwell respectively, and then Joshua had to shrug that off and head into an arena that crackled with expectation as master of ceremonies Michael Buffer introduced 'the big boys of boxing'.

At the opening bell, Johnson surprisingly kept his promise to fight with his hands down. He decided his reflexes would keep him safe and he slipped a left-right from Joshua in the opening seconds.

The opening Joshua was looking for presented itself when Johnson pushed out a slow jab.

Joshua smacked him flush on the chin with a fast counter right hand, knocking him on to his heels. The crowd screamed as Johnson back-pedalled frantically. He was able to escape Joshua's follow-up attack and once his senses and footing returned, sought to eat up a few seconds with an Ali shuffle. The crowd laughed, but Joshua stayed focused, kept jabbing.

He kept jabbing until he had Johnson where he wanted him in a corner of the ring and then he threw his right hand. It connected and he kept punching. Joshua pumped out lefts and rights until a short right hand connected cleanly and took Johnson's legs from under him. He grabbed the top rope and straightened himself instantly, but, ruling that the ropes had kept him up, referee Ian John-Lewis gave Johnson an eight count.

On its completion, Joshua went straight back on the attack.

Trapped on the ropes, Johnson tried to twist and turn away from the punches, but Joshua found gaps, pounded him towards the floor and then found a devastating short right uppercut. The punch dramatically laid out Johnson over the bottom rope – and then the bell rang.

The fight looked to be over.

Mitchell jumped into the ring and dragged the dazed Johnson back to his stool. Johnson told him he wanted to fight on and Mitchell did his best to revive him and lift his spirits. He threw water over him and told him, 'He's hit you with his best shot and you're still in there. Get through the next round and it will get easier.'

How much of that Johnson took in is impossible to say. Joshua had been punching him dizzy and he was surely still fuzzy-headed when the second round got under way.

Joshua knew he had Johnson hurt and close to defeat and he licked his lips with maniacal glee as he set about finishing him off. He missed with a lead right hand and then shrugged as if to say, 'It was worth a try,' a sign of how comfortable he felt.

There were signs that Johnson's head was clearing and he might get through the crisis – and then Joshua drove him to the ropes and jumped on him, pouring in punch after punch to convince the referee the time was right to halt the fight.

Joshua had taken only four minutes and 22 seconds to do what no heavyweight had done, a result that would get him noticed in America.

Fight No 14
Gary Cornish

At: The O2 Arena, Greenwich, London

On: Saturday, 12 September 2015

Opponent's record: Fights 21 Wins 21 Losses 0

Joshua's weight: 17st 11lb

Opponent's weight: 18st 4lb

Scheduled for: 12 rounds

WBC International heavyweight title, vacant Commonwealth heavyweight title

Result: Joshua won by first-round stoppage

THE WIN over Johnson propelled Joshua up to second in the WBC rankings – the title was held by Deontay Wilder – but rather than push on for a world title fight, Hearn decided to pull Joshua back.

There had to be more fights, and rounds, between these confidence-building knockovers and a world title challenge. There was a world-class quality and power to Joshua's punches, but after 13 fights, every other aspect of his boxing remained untested. What about his stamina? What happens when someone hits him back? What about his chin?

Hearn reckoned Dillian Whyte could supply answers to the above.

He was hard, full of fight – and Joshua–Whyte would sell. Whyte had a win over Joshua when they were novice amateurs and better still for Hearn, they didn't get on.

Hearn tried to make the fight for 12 September, but Whyte decided he needed a warm-up and he was put on the undercard of a fight between Joshua and Gary Cornish for Joshua's WBC International title and the vacant Commonwealth belt.

The plan was for Joshua to beat Cornish and Whyte to beat Brian Minto – and then the winners would meet later in the year.

The press conferences leading up to the show at the O2 Arena did what they were supposed to do.

They created plenty of interest in a fight between Joshua and Whyte.

Whyte, said Joshua, took drugs, a reference to his ban for, apparently unknowingly, taking the banned substance methylhexanamine (MHA).

Joshua, replied Whyte, sold them.

They would have to wait to get their hands on each other.

Whyte had to get past Minto and Joshua faced Cornish, a towering 28-year-old from Inverness in Scotland with a perfect 21-0 record.

He was taller than Joshua, around 6ft 7in, was likely to be heavier as well, but appeared to lack his punch and definitely his schooling.

Cornish took up boxing late having played football in the Highland League and only had nine amateur bouts, winning the Scottish ABA super-heavyweight title in 2010 before turning professional the following year. Expectations weren't that high. Not since Ken Shaw in 1950 had there been a Scot in domestic heavyweight contention.

Shaw, forced out of his British title eliminator against Freddie Mills with a back injury, was managed by Tommy Gilmour Sr and his son didn't have too much luck discovering a Scottish heavyweight contender either.

Gilmour Jr liked the look of Ian Millarvie for a spell before injury derailed a fighter he described as 'the most accident prone person I've ever met' and a few years later, along came Cornish.

Through Gilmour's connections, Cornish got some exposure on Sky Sports undercards where viewers saw a novice learning his trade against tough journeymen.

Cornish piled up wins by boxing steadily and patiently behind his jab.

Gilmour said he had a five-year plan for Cornish – and it didn't involve a meeting with Joshua.

Cornish took the fight against Gilmour's wishes.

He saw the value in keeping the zero at the end of Cornish's professional record, but had the confidence of an unbeaten fighter and was getting paid well. Though there was a shortage of sparring partners in Scotland, Cornish would be as well prepared as he could be.

He took six weeks off from his job as a joiner to train full time with no-nonsense coach Stevie McGuire.

McGuire had once walked out of his own son's corner because he wasn't following his instructions.

Cornish was a huge underdog.

He was a step or two down from Johnson in terms of experience, but he was fresh, ambitious and revealed a gunslinger's go-for-broke mentality when I spoke to him in his dressing room around an hour before the fight.

'Two big lads and anything could happen,' was his reading of the fight.

What happened was what was expected to happen.

Whyte had earlier slugged his way to a third-round stoppage of Brian Minto that wasn't universally well received by the crowd and they weren't glad to see Cornish either, booing him all the way to the ring.

He probably didn't need to watch a replay of all Joshua's knockouts on the big screen as he waited for his opponent to make his entrance, but Cornish wasn't intimidated and took the fight to Joshua at the bell.

Joshua later admitted he felt his jabs in the opening moments.

The first power punch was landed by Joshua. Cornish was stung by a left hook and looked for an immediate response. Joshua let a left-right from the Scot glance off his shoulder, then pushed off his back foot and drove a fast counter right hand through Cornish's wide open defences and on to his chin.

Cornish went down – and the crowd went crazy. He spent most of the eight count on one knee, got up, then set about fighting his way out of trouble.

Joshua went with Cornish when he started firing punches and hurt him in the exchanges. Cornish was dazed, tried to grab, but Joshua steadied him with a stiff jab, then clipped him with short left hooks that sent him to his knees.

This time, he only just beat the count, getting up at nine, and referee Victor Loughlin decided to wave the fight off after just one minute and 37 seconds.

Sky Sports were full of praise for Joshua and Cornish would later say he had been hit on the chin by a future world champion, but Whyte was less impressed.

He had seen weaknesses he was in no rush to share and added, 'I'm a machine, I don't fear any man. I'm going to put him in his place.'

Fight No 15
Dillian Whyte

At: The O2 Arena, Greenwich, London

On: Saturday, 12 December 2015

Opponent's record: Fights 16 Wins 16 Losses 0

Joshua's weight: 17st 7lb

Opponent's weight: 17st 5lb

Scheduled for: 12 Rounds

Vacant British heavyweight title, Commonwealth heavyweight title, WBC International heavyweight title

Result: Joshua won by seventh-round stoppage

'SOMETIMES I think I put myself through too much,' admitted Joshua.

'But this is what it is about, it is about giving it your best.

'If I keep on doing that, I am always going to get to the top, regardless of what I do. Regardless of if I am boxing or working in Starbucks.

'I am the tea boy in this place [Starbucks], but if I keep giving it my best, I am going to get to become a manager.

'I'm a boxer, I become Olympic champion and as a professional I want to become British and European champion and that just comes down to giving it my best.'

Joshua got the chance to become the British champion, and settle a score, in his 15th fight.

Hearn had done a good job building Joshua – and now he had to hang on to him.

He was under pressure to deliver him the sort of deal Al Haymon was offering fighters.

The reclusive former music mogul was investing millions in his Premier Boxing Champions series that had brought boxing back to free-to-air television in America – and Joshua was sure to be on his radar.

Hearn had to find a way to keep him.

He renegotiated Joshua's contract, Sky Sports made him a Scholar, a lucrative deal that involved a handful of public appearances, and his next contest, against Dillian Whyte, would be on pay-per-view.

To watch Joshua and Whyte settle their differences, Sky Sports subscribers would have to pay an extra £16.95 on top of their monthly subscription – and Joshua's share of every purchase would be £10.

There were those, *Boxing News* among them, who didn't think Joshua–Whyte deserved to be on pay-per-view, but the decision was justified by the public's desire to see the fight.

Tickets had reportedly sold out in six hours and with Sky Sports driving pay-per-view sales, 500,000 buys was a possibility, maybe more.

The rivalry between Whyte and Joyce had been simmering ever since they were novice amateurs.

Whyte actually made his boxing debut against Joshua, on a club show in 2009.

'My trainer couldn't find an opponent,' remembered Whyte, 'and then he told me there was this guy who had two fights and two knockouts.

'He wasn't sure whether he should make the fight because Anthony Joshua was supposed to be the next big thing.

'I told him, "I'm not like the other boys at the club, make the fight."

'Everyone was saying, "You're fighting Anthony Joshua? Are you sure? He's knocking everyone out and he's six foot this, six foot that."'

The fight went ahead – and Whyte won a clash of tough, willing novices on points.

Joshua took a standing count in the second round – and Whyte says that changed the fight.

After that, he said, Joshua was less willing to engage and that is why he went on to win the bout on points.

'It was my first boxing match ever so I was making a load of mistakes,' remembered Whyte, 'but I had power, heart and loved the fight. That's what made the difference. After the fight he just said, "You're too strong."'

In the build-up to their rematch six years later, Whyte found rather more significance in their amateur fight than Joshua did.

'I've been in his head for years,' said Whyte. Joshua replied the fight was long ago and meant nothing.

Whyte was angered by the way Joshua dismissed him in interviews.

Joshua told him to 'be professional about your career' and gave the impression he thought Whyte was not at his level and had manoeuvred himself into a big fight by dragging up a meaningless amateur club bout from years before.

There were feisty exchanges between them on social media and they had to be pulled apart after bumping into each other during a training camp with Wladimir Klitschko in Austria.

Kevin Johnson got between them and reasoned, 'Why do it for free?'

Joshua–Whyte was worth money and Hearn, and the others around Joshua, thought the time was right to make the fight towards the end of 2015.

Joshua was ranked in the top ten by all the four major governing bodies and the feeling was that if Hearn waited too much longer to make the fight, Joshua would have gone way beyond Whyte.

Joshua seemed to be heading for the world title, while rather less was expected of Whyte.

But he was expected to give Joshua a fight. Whyte was the tough opponent who would tell us more about Joshua.

Born in Jamaica, Whyte relocated to London in his teens and he grew up fast.

He was a father at 13, started working the doors of London nightclubs at 14 and those who knew him reckoned there were two Dillian Whytes.

He could be charming one moment – he called me 'sir' during interviews – and destructive the next.

The sensible thing to do, the only thing to do, when Whyte asks you to drink up and leave is to drink up and leave. The story went, he was once challenged by a crowd of rowdy revellers who didn't want to drink up and leave – and laid all ten of them out.

Upon leaving prison at 17, he started out as a kickboxer and after amateur boxing officials discovered he had competed at European level, they banned him.

Because of that, Whyte turned professional earlier than he anticipated, after just six amateur bouts, and learned under trainer Chris Okoh, the former Commonwealth cruiserweight champion.

Whyte showed in his early fights that he was big, strong and full of fight.

He made his intention to land the right hand a bit too obvious, but as his career went on, Whyte learned to set it up with a jab to the body that distracted his opponents.

Whyte won his first nine fights, then was handed a two-year suspension.

He was found to have methylhexanamine in his system after drinking Jack3D, an energy-boosting supplement available over the counter in health shops.

Whyte branded his ban 'a joke. I get two years for a drink.'

He stayed in the gym and, needing to find a new trainer after Okoh was injured in a car accident, he turned to

Johnathon Banks. He knew Banks from his training camps with Wladimir Klitschko.

At 33, Banks was young for a trainer. His career as a cruiserweight and heavyweight contender rather petered out and he took over training Klitschko following Emanuel Steward's death in 2012.

Two weeks before Joshua met Whyte, he had been in Klitschko's corner when Tyson Fury bamboozled him out of his belts, adding further interest to Joshua–Whyte.

The winner would be close to a shot at Fury.

The build-up to the fight was tense and when Joshua and Whyte came together at Sky Sports' studios in Isleworth for a *Gloves Are Off* promotional programme, there was a furious exchange – and Joshua was the instigator.

He made mention of Whyte's children while they sat across a table from each other and Whyte replied, 'Your sisters will be on my lap after the fight.'

Joshua was incensed, slammed his fists on the table and jumped to his feet.

Whyte smiled back at him and security stepped in.

Andy Brown is six feet tall, weighs around 16 stones and knew Whyte well enough to be able to reason with him. Whyte protested that Joshua had overstepped the mark. 'If you stay in this room,' Brown told him, 'the fight will be off. Let's go for a walk.'

Whyte took his advice and left the room for around 15 minutes before returning.

The fight would go ahead and as it drew closer, there were signs the public were believing in Whyte.

Bookmakers reported there was a lot of money placed on him in the days before the fight.

There was a feeling that Whyte's street toughness gave him the edge.

Nonsense, said Hearn.

'In boxing,' he explained, 'there are a lot of good people trying to be bad.

'Anthony Joshua is a bad guy trying to be good. From a PR perspective, he's fantastic. But when it's personal, in the ring, he's different. He wants to hurt Dillian Whyte, badly.'

Joshua seemed angered that because his public persona was rather more agreeable than Whyte's, he was somehow less of a fighting man.

'I'm not a celebrity,' Joshua told me with real meaning shortly after the Whyte bout was announced. 'I'm a fighter.'

Joshua fancied he had everything Whyte had – and more – and sparring partner Frazer Clarke gave an insight into the Joshua the public didn't see.

'We are both very competitive,' he said, 'and we've had some wild spars. He would hit me after the bell, I would hit him back and all hell would break loose. We would really go for each other and Robert McCracken would jump in and start shouting, "Pack it in you two."'

There were fears Joshua and Whyte would come to blows at the weigh-in, but Whyte kept his hands shoved in his pockets and the main talking point was Chris Eubank Sr's bizarre dancing.

His son, Chris Eubank Jr, was fighting on the undercard and beat eccentric Irishman Gary 'Spike' O'Sullivan, forcing a retirement after seven rounds.

Boxing News fancied Joshua would beat Whyte inside four rounds – and that soon looked like being a fair assessment.

For much of the first round, Whyte looked to be a clean punch away from defeat. Several times he wobbled and swayed, but he stayed on his feet – and fought back. The round was clearly Joshua's and he let go another punch after the bell sounded.

Whyte was furious and as referee Howard Foster got between the fighters, Whyte reached around him and aimed a left hook at Joshua.

Both corners and security spilled into the ring, but Whyte was still able to launch another punch at Joshua that missed, before Banks dragged him to his corner.

Foster admitted afterwards that on another occasion, both fighters would have been disqualified, but he took the magnitude of the fight into account and settled for giving both a warning before the second round got under way.

During that second round, Joshua was only one clean punch from defeat.

Whyte started the round positively, leading off with jabs that appeared to amuse Joshua.

He set about putting Whyte in his place with combinations that were half blocked – and then found a clean right hand that knocked Whyte on to his heels.

He stumbled back to the ropes, Joshua unloaded and Whyte lashed back with a short left hook.

The punch slammed off Joshua's jaw and his legs stiffened dramatically.

Whyte's eyes widened. He knew this was his chance – and he went for it. He slung around a dozen punches at Joshua that had everything behind them – and they all missed.

Joshua regained his senses quickly enough and every follow-up swing Whyte hurled at him, he saw coming and either blocked or dodged.

But Joshua did appear to feel a body punch in the closing seconds of a round that was emphatically Whyte's.

The third was his as well. Joshua looked tired. He struggled to let his hands go in the opening minute of the round, allowing Whyte to outwork him, and when he did start throwing punches in the second half of the round, they were slow and laboured.

Whyte slipped them and whacked away at Joshua's body.

This was the test Joshua had been asking for and it looked like he might not come through it.

He appeared to be unravelling.

But it was a very different Joshua who came out for the fourth round.

The speed and venom was back in his punches and though Whyte fired back to stay in the fight, he mostly missed and took some heavy blows to his body.

Joshua looked to be in control and there were anxious cries of, 'You've got the heart, Dee,' from Whyte's supporters gathered near his corner when it got tough for him in the fifth.

Whyte tried to rally in the sixth and finally, he landed the right hand he had been looking for from the start of the fight.

The punch just bounced off Joshua and when he landed his right hand in the seventh, Whyte came apart. The whipping punch caught Whyte behind his ear – and it sent shockwaves through his body. He zigged and zagged crazily, his body out of control, and as he struggled to pull himself together, Joshua wore what commentator Nick Halling called 'a wolf-like grin'.

Whyte got his hands up to block a left and then two rights, but stumbled into the path of a right uppercut.

The punch lifted Whyte off his feet and he landed on the second rope.

The referee hurriedly steered Joshua to a neutral corner before kneeling down to take out Whyte's gum shield.

The fight was over – even if Whyte didn't think so.

He was still trying to get to his feet after the fight was waved off.

'It was about bragging rights,' said Joshua afterwards, 'and who's the man.'

Fight No 16
Charles Martin

At: The O2 Arena, Greenwich, London

On: Saturday, 9 April 2016

Opponent's record: Fights 24 Wins 23 Losses 0 Draws 1

Joshua's weight: 17st 6lb

Opponent's weight: 17st 7lb

Result: Joshua won by second-round stoppage

JOSHUA TOLD me before he fought Whyte that he might challenge for world honours 'sooner than you think' – and that's how it turned out.

The moody Dereck Chisora, a former British, Commonwealth and European champion who had twice been soundly beaten by Tyson Fury, was approached to fight Joshua for the vacant European heavyweight title on Saturday, 9 April.

Terms couldn't be agreed and Sam Sexton started a social media campaign to get the fight with Joshua.

Sexton was an honest former Commonwealth champion from Norwich who had struggled with injuries, but Hearn was thinking bigger.

He sent Joshua a text message suggesting a world title fight against IBF champion 'King' Charles Martin.

'Let's roll,' was Joshua's instant reply.

Martin was considered fortunate to hold a world title.

Tyson Fury bamboozled Wladimir Klitschko out of the WBA Super, IBF and WBO belts in Dusseldorf in November 2015 and three days later, the IBF ordered him to defend against mandatory challenger Vyacheslav Glaskov, with purse bids due within a few days.

Unable to meet that unreasonable demand, Fury was stripped and the IBF paired Glaskov with their next highest ranked heavyweight.

Martin had answered an advertisement to become a fighter.

'Wanted,' it read, 'the next American heavyweight great, must be at least 6ft 3in, more than 230lb, no experience needed.'

Michael King was behind All-American Heavyweights.

He was a television executive keen to invest the fortunes he made making *The Oprah Winfrey Show* into trying to regain American dominance of the heavyweight championship.

There was a seven-and-a-half-year gap between Shannon Briggs losing the WBO title to Sultan Ibragimov and Deontay Wilder seizing the WBC belt from Bermane Stiverne in January 2015.

'It wasn't just that the US slipped,' said former *Ring* editor and Hall of Fame writer Steve Farhood, 'the rest of the world caught up.

'The rest of the world seems hungrier. Trainers tell me that fighters from other parts of the world are hungrier and if you're a big athlete in America, you have more options. Basketball and American football might be more lucrative. Boxing is such a hard sport. It takes such discipline and sacrifice.'

Wilder looked like he could be the heavyweight America was waiting for. He was a boisterous character with a big punch and a good story. Wilder was inspired by his daughter, Naieya, who was battling spina bifida, a birth defect of the brain and spine.

He won bronze at the 2008 Olympics in Beijing and though *Boxing News* described him as 'crude' and suggested that unless he tidied up his boxing, he would come unstuck before he got to world level, Wilder kept chinning everyone put in front of him until he challenged Bermane Stiverne for the WBC title in January 2015.

Boxing with a broken right hand from the early rounds, Wilder won unanimously on points.

The other belts were held by Aussie brawler Lucas Browne, the WBA 'regular' champion, and Martin.

At the time he read that advertisement for a heavyweight champion, Martin was a 23-year-old construction worker from Phoenix, Arizona, who had played basketball at college and spent some time in prison for dealing drugs.

He had started boxing in his late teens, had a handful of amateur bouts – and was accepted.

'I was an amateur,' said Martin of his time in the system, 'but I didn't have to do anything but box. I was blessed to be in a school that paid for everything. We got salaries, accommodation: all we had to do was box. I hadn't boxed until I was 19. Then I was getting my foot into it, doing a sparring session here and there. Then, at 23, boxing chose me.'

He had 65 amateur bouts in total and turned professional after reaching the 2012 Golden Gloves final, losing on points to Andrew Coleman.

The 23 wins on his 24-fight professional record – there was a draw early in his career – didn't mean an awful lot, including his win for the vacant IBF championship.

Glaskov's right knee gave way in the third round, leaving him unable to continue, and without landing a meaningful, clean blow, Martin was the champion.

The crowd's boos drowned out a post-fight interview that revealed Martin to be rather eccentric, childlike even.

Even though Martin was considered fortuitous to win the belt, and for some pundits he was possibly one of the worst world heavyweight champions in recent history, there were still concerns the fight had come too soon for Joshua, in only his 16th fight and after two and a half years as a professional.

The record books showed that only Leon Spinks (eighth), Michael Bentt (12th), James J. Corbett (13th) and James J. Jeffries (14th) had won a version of the world heavyweight championship in fewer fights.

Hearn's thinking was that if Martin wasn't a world champion, he would have happily taken the fight and, as for the fear that winning the IBF belt would take Joshua to a level he wasn't yet ready for, the top two spots in the IBF rankings were vacant, meaning that, should Joshua win, he could milk the belt with maybe a couple of soft voluntary defences before facing a stiffer mandatory.

Martin told the British press he had other options. Olympian Dominic Breazeale and faded gunslinger Chris Areola were mooted as possible challengers, but explained, 'Winning this fight will change my life. It will turn me into a superstar. I want people to know me like they know [top pound-for-pound boxer] Floyd [Mayweather Jr].'

More importantly, the Joshua fight was by far the most lucrative option. Hearn was rumoured to be paying him $3.5m to fight Joshua – and nobody else was going to pay Martin that sort of money.

He was the IBF heavyweight champion, but that didn't mean Martin was marketable.

Fury, the complex man-child only happy when he's making headlines, piped up and accused Hearn of buying the belt for Joshua, but Joshua had the requisite ranking and Hearn had the money and television backing to make it happen.

That's how professional boxing works.

Boxing Monthly editor Graham Houston compared Joshua challenging Martin with fights such as James J.

Braddock–Joe Louis and Trevor Berbick–Mike Tyson, clashes when the heavyweight championship was expected to change hands, possibly marking the start of a new era for the division.

Doubters pointed out that Joshua had yet to face a southpaw as a professional and as an amateur, Romanian left-hander Mihai Nistor stopped him in the quarter-finals of the European Championships in 2011.

Supporters remembered Joshua had twice outpointed Roberto Cammarelle as an amateur.

To prepare for Martin, Joshua sparred southpaws Joey Abell, Lenroy Thomas and Otto Wallin, an unbeaten Swede he beat in the amateurs.

'Sparring is the key,' Joshua told the press, 'and I've been blessed to have three southpaws over the last six to eight weeks.

'Early on, I was getting caught by the back hand a bit, but I was soon defending it, slipping it, countering it.'

Tickets for Martin–Joshua were soon snapped up, 90 seconds was all it took according to Hearn's publicity department, and in the States, Joshua would be shown for the first time, on Showtime Boxing International Live.

'There was tremendous interest among hardcore fans in the States,' said Farhood. 'Joshua was supposed to be the real thing.'

Joshua looked like the real thing at the weigh-in: a superbly sculpted 17st 6lb, while Martin was a rather more fleshy 17st 7lb – and in playful mood.

After the weigh-in, Martin pulled faces for selfies – Mike Tyson he wasn't – while around him, everyone wondered how long he would last.

One or two rounds was the guess of most.

The bookmakers agreed, while Martin said that, having never been hurt before, he could absorb whatever Joshua threw at him, take him into the later rounds and beat him.

Joshua envisaged a straightforward win. 'If I do what I do, it's a routine stop off in that ring,' he said. 'I go into the ring, get the win, hurt someone and everyone cheers.'

He said he had learned from the Whyte bout and that this time, there would be no such drama.

'I'll be a lot smarter,' he said. 'If I fight that way, it's very entertaining, I will catch you sooner or later, but if I steam in without worrying what's coming back, that's dangerous.

'I have to establish myself before I put my presence on him.'

Feverish anticipation swept around the O2 Arena the following night, when, dressed in a white robe, Joshua made his way to the ring.

Once there, he leaned into the ropes, shook his huge, muscular arms loose and acknowledged friends at ringside, while, dressed in a long gown and with a cheap-looking cardboard crown perched on his head, Martin made his entrance.

Martin said he would beat Joshua with movement and at the opening bell, he circled anxiously, not throwing much.

The punch Joshua was looking for was the straight right hand and in the opening round, he couldn't land it cleanly.

He fell short a few times, to shrieks from the excitable crowd, but in the second, he got his feet an inch or two closer and his timing right. Martin jabbed, Joshua let his right hand go – and the champion hit the floor.

Martin sat on the canvas wondering how he ended up there. He would later say he didn't see Joshua's right hand, but quickly gathered his senses and took most of referee Jean-Pierre Van Imschoot's eight count on one knee.

The fight went on and moments later, there was a repeat.

Joshua used Martin's jab to find his range again and drilled him with another hard right down the middle that put him on the seat of his trunks.

Joshua strolled to a neutral corner, smiling and shrugging a shrug that said, 'What did you expect? This is what I do,' while Martin did a passable impression of a fighter who wanted to beat the count.

He timed his rise to coincide with the referee reaching the count of ten and the fight was over, after four minutes and 32 seconds.

'He didn't want to get up,' said Joshua afterwards. 'I don't blame him.'

The second shortest reign in heavyweight history – just 85 days – was over and Britain had an eighth world heavyweight champion after Bob Fitzsimmons, Lennox Lewis, Michael Bentt, Herbie Hide, Frank Bruno, Henry Akinwande and David Haye.

Joshua wanted to share the moment with everyone and for more than an hour after Martin was counted out, the new champion was still signing autographs and posing for photographs.

Beating Martin inside two rounds meant Joshua won the world heavyweight championship in just 34 rounds as a professional, fewer than anyone else, and the straightforward manner of his win left him feeling 'a bit underwhelmed' and as ever, he was keen to look forward.

'I want to fight the big names,' he explained. 'You're only as good as who you fight.

'In the UK, I have to become the hottest prospect, so that means fighting the likes of [Tyson] Fury, David Price, [Dereck] Chisora and David Haye.

'Beat all these guys, they can't say anything bad about me anymore and then move on.

'Then we have guys like Bryant Jennings, Bermane Stiverne, Luis Ortiz, Malik Scott, go through that. [Alexander] Ustinov, [Kubrat] Pulev, [Ruslan] Chagaev. These are the guys I want to start putting on my record.'

The big fight was with Fury, who took to Twitter moments after Martin was counted out to brand Joshua 'ponderous' and 'slow like a bodybuilder. Let me slay the lamb.'

First Fury had to get through Wladimir Klitschko in their rematch on 9 July, ironically the date Hearn had pencilled in for Joshua's first defence of the IBF title.

Ron Lewis wrote in *The Times* that Fury–Joshua 'is becoming a clash for the heart of the sport, between casual fans and the hardcore support. Fury demands respect after beating a great champion, but Joshua is the darling of a celebrity culture and hero to fans who just want to see a punch-up. Debates about who is the most deserving will continue until they meet in the ring.'

Fight No 17
Dominic Breazeale

At: The O2 Arena, Greenwich, London

On: Saturday, 25 June 2016

Opponent's record: Fights 17 Wins 17 Losses 0

Joshua's weight: 17st 5lb

Opponent's weight: 18st 3lb

Scheduled for: 12 Rounds

IBF heavyweight title

Result: Joshua won by seventh-round stoppage

JOSHUA started boxing when he was 18 years old, won Olympic gold at 22 and by 26, he was the heavyweight champion of the world.

The next four years, and more, would be spent building his legacy.

'I don't see myself losing,' he told *The Sun* in the afterglow of the Martin thrashing.

'I want to go on until I'm 35 – I want to maintain this for a decade.'

Joshua wasn't satisfied by winning the IBF title, the same way he wasn't satisfied by winning Olympic gold.

The belt wasn't the pinnacle for him, it was another platform.

There had been world heavyweight champions who had reigned briefly and been largely forgotten, British fighters like Henry Akinwande and Herbie Hide among them, and Joshua didn't want that.

He wanted to press on, be recognised as the best heavyweight in the world and leave a legacy.

He said he would 'keep my challenger's mindset, never put myself on a pedestal' and at a fresh 26 years old, he had the time, and the opponents, to leave a mark on boxing history.

Possible opponents included Tyson Fury, Deontay Wilder and Wladimir Klitschko and Joshua seemed to accept they were ahead of him.

Fury would meet Klitschko two weeks after Joshua's first defence – or so we thought – and the hope was Joshua would face the winner by the end of the year.

Then there was Joseph Parker, an unbeaten 24-year-old New Zealander.

Five weeks after Joshua took the IBF belt off Martin, Parker had become his mandatory challenger with a points win over Carlos Takam.

Parker was a highly regarded young puncher who appeared to have the same gunslinger's mentality as Joshua and the promise of seeing Joshua face such opponents led to US broadcasters Showtime offering him a lucrative multi-fight deal.

'The immediate question is, "Why would an American network do this deal now?"' said Stephen Espinoza, Showtime Sports executive vice-president and general manager.

'It's a combination of several factors. One, obviously Anthony's talent, his charisma and his skills.

'Two, as importantly, neither Eddie nor Anthony have any timidity about taking tough fights.'

Joshua could squeeze in a voluntary defence, possibly two, before facing Parker and Showtime were keen to see him against an American challenger.

Dominic Breazeale, a 30-year-old from Anaheim, California, was 17-0 (15 knockouts) and had the requisite ranking. Well, he did after the fight was announced, jumping up four places in the IBF rankings to number nine.

He stood a lofty 6ft 7in tall and like Joshua, Breazeale fought in the London Olympics, going out in his first contest to the Russian, Magomed Omarov, 19-8.

Breazeale stayed to watch the final between Joshua and Cammarelle and left before the decision was announced, convinced that the Italian had won, but that the verdict would not go his way.

'I do not believe Anthony Joshua is a gold medallist,' Breazeale told the press after the Joshua fight was announced. 'Cammarelle won that fight.'

Breazeale says that fight convinced him London judges weren't to be trusted when he challenged Joshua.

'It's his jungle, his promotion, his judges,' he said. 'I know this fight cannot be allowed to go the distance.

'I have to bully him and knock him out. I say I will in about eight rounds.'

That was a view not shared by many. Breazeale's world title credentials were creaky.

He had been fed mostly old journeymen and fat cruiserweights in his professional career and he had a desperate struggle against Amir Mansour, a 43-year-old ex-convict he outweighed by a hefty 44lb.

In the third round, Breazeale was knocked off his feet by a sweeping southpaw right hook.

He toughed it out when Mansour threw everything at him in a bid to finish the fight and by the end of the round, Mansour had punched himself out.

He retired on his stool after five rounds after his tongue was ripped open, needing 36 stitches to repair.

Because of that performance, Breazeale was largely written off as a future heavyweight champion.

Breazeale had been a promising American footballer. He was a quarterback at the University of Northern Colorado and was hoping for a chance in the National Football League, but a friend persuaded him that given his size, athleticism and toughness he should try boxing.

At 23 years old, Breazeale went to the gym and said, 'I just had natural ability.

'Boxing has always been in my blood. My dad did it and my two uncles. I never knew they were boxing at the time they boxed, but later they told me boxing stories and that kind of got me hooked.'

With his wife pregnant, Breazeale sensed boxing was a chance to make money for his family.

Like Charles Martin, he was part of the All-American Heavyweights programme and as an amateur, Breazeale won the US super-heavyweight title and reached the final of an Olympic qualifier in Brazil to book his trip to London.

Four years later, he returned to London to face Joshua and irritated him when they met at a press conference by refusing to shake his hand.

'Have you got a problem?' asked Joshua.

'The problem's in front of you.'

Joshua pursued the problem, questioned Breazeale's street-fighting credentials, and made him back down.

Others who dealt with Breazeale found him rather more agreeable, though comparisons with Charles Martin made him tetchy.

He reckoned Martin only came to London for the money and that he expected to be knocked out.

'The only thing we have in common,' he protested, 'is we're both American.'

Breazeale made flattering comparisons between himself and Riddick Bowe, but the truth was, even in America, he wasn't considered a future champion and the expectation was, he would last about as long as Martin did.

Critics pointed out that though Breazeale was a good size – an inch taller than Joshua – and possessed a long, solid jab, his punches didn't flow, his feet were slow and his defences leaky. The feeling was that if Mansour, an old cruiserweight who just put his head down and slung big back hands, could drop him, Joshua surely could knock him out.

The interest here was Joshua and Breazeale was largely anonymous at his own weigh-in.

He didn't have the gang of backslappers that Martin brought with him, just his wife and one of their young sons, and stood on his own, arms folded, in the Earls Court sunshine in the minutes before the weigh-in.

Had the gathering crowd recognised Breazeale, they would have surely taunted him, but they didn't.

The following night, Joshua was straight down to business. In the opening seconds, he threw a fast left hook that whistled just past Breazeale's chin and he kept fast, heavy punches coming in twos and threes.

Breazeale tried to jab his way into the fight and Joshua took his best punch away from him. Every time Breazeale jabbed in the opening round, he missed and a split second later, a right hand came fizzing back.

That made him think twice about throwing his jab and instead, Breazeale got his hands up and looked to block and counter. But he didn't block everything Joshua threw and his counter punches were off target.

Breazeale just stood in front of Joshua, taking a steady beating. He stumbled late in the second after Joshua connected with a combination of short, jolting punches and went back to his stool at the bell with a swelling around his right eye.

Breazeale proved he was stubborn and had a good chin, but he didn't seem to have any way of turning the fight his way. The punches he was shipping were taking something out of him and with every round, the damage around his right eye worsened.

Breazeale still had his pride, however, and at the bell to end the sixth, he briefly blocked Joshua's path to his corner and glared at him.

Early in the seventh, Breazeale took the fight to Joshua for the first time in the fight and clipped him with a right hand and left hook.

The champion responded by opening up with a burst that knocked Breazeale on to his heels.

This time, Joshua sensed he was ready to be knocked out, so kept punching until Breazeale hit the floor.

His pride got him off the floor at the referee's count of seven and Joshua was soon all over him.

He knocked Breazeale back into the ropes with a hard jab, manoeuvred him into a corner and unloaded.

Breazeale tried to fight his way out of trouble and was clobbered to the canvas, referee Howard Foster waving the fight off instantly, without starting to count.

Joshua was still the IBF heavyweight champion and looking forward to a break.

'I only had two weeks off after my last fight,' said Joshua, who revealed he battled glandular fever in the build-up to the fight.

'Now I want to have a nice bit of time to rest. I'm tired and I'm working hard. Now I can recharge my batteries and start again.'

Fight No 18
Eric Molina

At: The Manchester Arena

On: Saturday, 10 December 2016

Opponent's record: Fights 28 Wins 25 Losses 3

Joshua's weight: 17st 11lb

Opponent's weight: 16st 13.5lb

Scheduled for: 12 Rounds

IBF heavyweight title

Result: Joshua won by third-round stoppage

THE HOPE was that Joshua would meet Wladimir Klitschko in Manchester on 10 December.

Klitschko was looking for a fight after Tyson Fury pulled out of their rematch for a second time, but for a number of reasons, negotiations were difficult and then Klitschko was injured and the bout collapsed.

Hughie Fury turned down £600,000 to fight Joshua and either David Price or Eric Molina was expected to step up.

They had been matched together in an eliminator on the undercard.

Price, a towering Liverpudlian who had won a bronze medal at the 2008 Olympics in Beijing, did his best to get the fight by retelling the story of how he had flattened Joshua during a sparring session.

Price hoped that would create interest in the fight, but ended up believing that went against him after Joshua's handlers went for Molina, a 34-year-old schoolteacher from Weslaco, Texas, who taught children with special needs and was best known for losing in nine rounds to Deontay Wilder in a challenge for the WBC title the previous summer.

Price said Joshua, or rather his handlers, had taken 'the safer option'.

He explained to *Boxing News*, 'The reason why I would have been a better opponent than Molina is that I would have been going to win.

'Molina is not going to come to win. He's coming to mess [around with] Joshua and spoil for a few rounds, then he's going to sit on the ropes and get knocked out.

'I would have fought fire with fire.'

Molina was also, the rumours went, the cheaper option.

The news Joshua would defend against Molina was met with mostly groans by the boxing press and public, but Molina could punch and the history of heavyweight boxing proves that a no-hoper who can punch always has a chance against an under-motivated favourite.

Oliver McCall and Hasim Rahman both upset Lennox Lewis when his mind was elsewhere and Molina punched hard enough to stiffen Wilder's legs briefly in the third round before being belted out in the ninth.

'I will hit Anthony Joshua harder than he's ever been hit,' promised Molina. 'I will not sit back like I sat back against Wilder, I will attack.

'Every single fighter I've ever been in with, I've hurt.

'I don't fear Joshua. He has never before fought anyone like me, someone who can hit and hurt him at any single moment during the fight. We're going to see Joshua and his heart and chin tested.'

Molina had proved his heart and chin, and that he carries his power into the later rounds, with a dramatic come-from-behind win over former world light-heavyweight and cruiserweight champion Tomasz Adamek that took him to eighth in the IBF rankings and made him eligible for a shot at Joshua.

After nine of the 12 rounds, 39-year-old Adamek, fighting in front of his Polish fans in Krakow, had boxed his way into an 88-83 points lead on all three scorecards.

But in the tenth he started to look tired, Molina came on and found a right hand that sent Adamek crashing on to his back. He didn't beat the count.

The other key results on Molina's 28-fight record were a pair of one-round defeats.

Molina lost his professional debut inside a round, way back in 2007, and was handed a first-round defeat by ill-disciplined contender Chris Arreola, a result he explained by saying he 'only had three weeks to get ready and aside from that, I wasn't right mentally for that fight'.

He added, 'I'm much better now, a totally different fighter. If they [the critics and Joshua's team] are judging by that only, they are in for a big surprise.

'Now I'm bigger, in better condition and I'm stronger, and I have the experience, not just in fights, but in sparring big guys in the gym.'

Nonetheless, *Boxing News* expected Joshua to get rid of him early.

Editor Matt Christie even questioned whether Joshua–Molina was worthy of pay-per-view.

Pay-per-view, he reasoned, was for 50-50 fights and, by his reckoning, this was a 95-5 fight.

Christie also accepted that Joshua against anyone was now a big fight, more than that, a big event, and anyway, there was a fight on the undercard that promised to be rather more competitive.

Hearn matched combustible heavyweights Dereck Chisora and Dillian Whyte against each other, but the fight almost didn't happen.

During a press conference, Chisora erupted after Whyte threatened him – and threw a table at him.

The British Boxing Board of Control held an emergency meeting before deciding the fight could go ahead.

For the first time in his professional career, Joshua would have Robert McCracken in his corner. McCracken had been advising Joshua since he had turned professional and was presumably brought in to help take his career to the next level.

McCracken said Joshua enjoyed training – 'It's never an issue getting him to the gym,' he told reporters – and still had much to learn.

'He's got the power,' said McCracken, 'but he obviously needs the smarts as well over 12 rounds against solid opposition.

'He's got to flow better, he has to show better control in the ring in pressure situations, his rhythm has to be better, not get over-excited when he has success, not get drawn into brawls when he doesn't need to.

'There's a lot to improve on, but he is working on that.'

McCracken was keen to point out Joshua had only been a professional for three years, had yet to go beyond seven rounds and was 'not the finished article yet'.

The big story of the week was broken by *The Sun* in the days before the fight.

If Joshua beat Molina, a near certainty according to every bookmaker, he would then fight Klitschko at Wembley Stadium on Saturday, 29 April 2017.

There was no comment from Hearn or Matchroom and, from Klitschko's manager Bernd Bonte, there was just an admission that talks were ongoing.

The rumour was Klitschko would be at ringside and the fight would be announced once Joshua had disposed of Molina.

Molina found hope in the rumour that Lawrence Okolie had dropped Joshua during sparring and promised to make him 'dance'. That is, he would hit Joshua so hard, he would lose control of his body, the way Whyte had 'danced' after

Joshua belted him with that right hand in the seventh round of their fight.

This fighting talk put a smile on Joshua's face. He replied that he would make Molina look like 'a novice'.

Molina looked, to one hardened observer at the weigh-in at a chilly Victoria Warehouse in Manchester, like 'another soft American' – and Joshua–Molina did look sure to be the least competitive world heavyweight title fight that day.

Earlier that day in Auckland, unbeaten pair Joseph Parker and Andy Ruiz met for the vacant WBO title.

Parker had been the mandatory challenger for Joshua's IBF title, but was also highly ranked with the WBO and decided a fight with Ruiz on home turf in New Zealand was preferable to a trip to London to face Joshua.

The 24-year-old won a close, majority decision over the chubby, quick-fisted Ruiz – had Ruiz won the last round, the fight would have been a draw – to announce himself, maybe not quite in the way he would have wanted, as another possible force in the post-Klitschko era.

Hours later, the attention switched to Manchester and a fight that unfolded pretty much how it was expected to unfold.

Whyte–Chisora lived up to expectations, Whyte winning a disputed split decision on the scorecards after ten rounds of non-stop slugging, and Joshua–Molina lived down to expectations.

From the opening bell, Joshua was purposeful behind his jab and Molina sat on the back foot, trying to keep himself safe without even thinking about throwing anything back.

Joshua kept him under pressure without landing too much cleanly until the final minute of the round when

Molina clearly felt a left hook. The second round was much like the first apart from that early in the session, Molina let go a couple of half-hearted right hands that fell harmlessly short.

Joshua put him back on the defensive with solid jabs and late in the round penetrated his defences with a three-punch combination that had Molina back-pedalling and wiping his nose.

There was no urgency from Joshua to finish the fight then, but after Molina stumbled after shipping a right hand in the third, he started to put full power into his punches.

Trapped in his own corner, Molina blocked a few blows on his arms and gloves before Joshua spotted a gap and drove a right hand through it. The punch detonated on Molina's chin and he crumpled to the floor.

He looked thoroughly fed up as he lay there and though this looked a hopeless cause, he got up, possibly on the insistence of his cornermen who were shouting in his ear, at the count of seven.

The end was only seconds away.

Joshua pounced on Molina and blasted him with left hooks that robbed him of his senses and left him flopped over the top rope and turning away, convincing referee Steve Gray to jump in.

It had been no sort of contest.

Joshua's next fight promised to be much tougher. As expected, Klitschko joined Joshua in the ring to officially announce their fight and refreshingly, there was no animosity between them.

'I've got respect for you,' Joshua told Klitschko, 'but this is competition.'

Fight No 19
Wladimir Klitschko

At: Wembley Stadium

On: Saturday, 29 April 2017

Opponent's record: Fights 68 Wins 64 Losses 4

Joshua's weight: 17st 12lb

Opponent's weight: 17st 2.25lb

Scheduled for: 12 Rounds

IBF heavyweight title, WBA Super world heavyweight title

Result: Joshua won by 11th-round stoppage

ONCE THE British press had finished quizzing him during a media day at his training camp in Austria, Klitschko had a question for them.

Was Joshua, he wanted to know, another Frank Bruno – or another Lennox Lewis?

Joshua, Klitschko was saying, still had much to prove. A couple of decades earlier, Bruno had benefited from being in the right place at the right time to win the world heavyweight title at the fourth attempt, taking the WBC belt off Oliver McCall in 1995.

McCall and Charles Martin would feature prominently in many writers' lists of weakest heavyweight champions in history and though Joshua kept his title longer than Bruno, beating Dominic Breazeale and Eric Molina hadn't proved much.

They certainly hadn't proved he was the new Lennox Lewis.

Lewis was the dominant heavyweight of his era and as former *Ring* magazine editor Steve Farhood put it, 'He changed the way America viewed British heavyweights.'

Klitschko spotted great potential in Joshua and said that in three years, he would possibly be too much for him, the implication being he was beatable now.

That was part of the mind games obviously, but there were doubts in Joshua's camp as well.

McCracken admitted afterwards that initially he thought the Klitschko fight had come 'three or four fights early' before deciding it was a risk worth taking.

The rewards were there. Hearn believed that with Floyd Mayweather apparently retired, beating Klitschko would make Joshua 'probably the biggest star in world boxing'.

That was a huge reward for beating a 41-year-old who hadn't fought for 17 months. No fighter, the thinking was in the Joshua camp, and not even a heavyweight, is in their prime at 41.

Klitschko believed the experience he had gained in a professional career that started when Joshua was just seven years old gave him the edge, but pointed out 'momentum and timing' were also crucial in deciding the outcome of a fight – and Joshua had those advantages.

Klitschko concluded that it was a '50-50 fight' – and the whole world wanted to watch it.

Wembley Stadium was a 90,000 sell-out, matching the crowd that saw Len Harvey and Jock McAvoy fight at White Hart Lane months before the start of the Second World War in 1939, and *The Sun*'s David Kidd went as far as to describe Joshua–Klitschko as 'an authentic fight to stop the planet – the brightest young heavyweight on Earth against the veteran who has dominated the division for a decade and is desperate to win back his crown'.

For Joshua it was 'just another fight, man. If I beat him I'm great, if I lose they will say, "He's a hype job."

'You can't get carried away. You beat Klitschko, then they'll say, "You've got to fight David Haye, then [Luis] Ortiz, then [Tyson] Fury comes out of retirement and then you've got to do it all over again."'

Klitschko had been doing just that for years, perhaps too long.

There had been signs of decline when he outpointed Bryant Jennings and then came the loss to Tyson Fury.

Fury didn't exactly dominate Klitschko, but with his size and head-scratching unorthodoxy, he stopped him doing much. Stats showed Klitschko landed only 86 punches throughout the fight, an average of around seven per round.

The rematch was set for July, then October, but Fury fell apart, admitting using cocaine to help his battles with depression.

What did the Fury fight prove?

The temptation was to say it proved Klitschko was finished, but with his size and mobility, Fury may well have always caused him problems. There were other explanations. Perhaps Klitschko was lacking motivation? Perhaps he just got old?

'It woke me up,' Klitschko told the British press when reflecting on the Fury fight.

'I prefer to go into this fight with AJ with experience and motivation that I got from Fury – my failure in that fight.

'I realise after so many years that I was not as motivated.'

Ahead of the Joshua fight, reports from Klitschko's training camp varied.

Johnny Nelson, the former WBO cruiserweight champion working for Sky Sports, said Klitschko looked good, but others weren't so sure.

Richard Towers was well placed to pick a winner having sparred both Klitschko and Joshua.

The retired Sheffield heavyweight reckoned Klitschko, who he described as 'the most competitive man on earth', had seen off many fighters like Joshua before, 'fighters who come forward in straight lines looking to land the right hand', and fancied he would win in the later rounds.

Klitschko winning late was one of two ways the fight would go, according to most pundits. Either that, or Joshua would win the fight in the early rounds.

Joshua was training for a quick knockout.

In Sheffield, he was setting about sparring partners Joe Joyce and Lawrence Okolie.

Okolie, an Olympian in Rio the previous summer making his way in the pros under Joshua's management, remembered the spars with a shake of the head. 'It was tough, man,' he said.

'If you let Klitschko get going and he gets that jab going and he starts pushing and shoving and looking for that right hand, then he's a real, real handful,' explained Robert McCracken in *Boxing News* the week before the fight.

Klitschko had based himself in the Austrian Alps with Johnathon Banks and had films of Joshua's fights shown repeatedly on video screens at the gym.

The other video he watched was of his loss to Lamon Brewster in 2004. Hearing the commentators write him off drove him on.

Banks knew the sort of talk that drove Klitschko on.

'I'll tell him, "Let's do another round," he'd look at me and I'd say, "What? You don't have it no more?"

'"No, yeah, I do."'

Win or lose against Joshua, Klitschko's place in heavyweight history was secure.

Over the previous 15 years or so he had two spells as world heavyweight champion, making 23 successful title defences and having a record 28 world heavyweight title fights, more than Joe Louis (27).

This was no golden era, but Klitschko and older brother Vitali had dominated it. Wladimir seldom lost rounds during his second spell as heavyweight champion and beat eight fighters who had held versions of the heavyweight title, fighters such as David Haye and Alexander Povetkin.

The turning point in Klitschko's career was when South African southpaw Corrie Sanders blasted him out in two rounds to take away his WBO title in 2003.

Following that fight, Klitschko brought in Emanuel Steward to help train him and though there was another loss to Lamon Brewster, Steward would reinvent him.

As the head of the Kronk gym in Detroit, Steward had masterminded the career of Thomas Hearns and got the best out of other fighters, such as Lennox Lewis and Dennis Andries, who came to him.

Steward got Klitschko boxing to his strengths – using his 81-inch reach to control the range – and tightened his defences.

Klitschko would joke he had a glass chin and to protect it, Steward got him taking half steps back, deflecting punches off his shoulders, moving around in circles, not back in straight lines.

Steward described once what made Klitschko so hard to beat.

'Wladimir is a master at controlling the ring,' he said. 'He makes you fight the way he wants you to fight.

'You think you're going to move around and outspeed him with your legs, but he cuts the ring off.

'You want to fight on the inside? He doesn't fight on the inside, but you can't either. He's going to make you stay at a distance and keep controlling you with that magic left hand.'

By the time Steward died in October 2012 at 68 years old, Klitschko had been the world's leading heavyweight for around six years and with Banks in his corner, he kept dominating.

'All I have to do,' explained Banks, 'is pour water on the seeds Manny has sown.'

Klitschko was always looking for ways to improve, always chasing perfection.

'It's very simple to get into a fight and throw punches,' he said once.

'But not to get caught, not to get hit once and eventually to knock your opponent out, that's the art of boxing. It's very difficult to accomplish. But it's possible.'

Joshua knew that wasn't what the crowd wanted to see.

'They want to see me get battered for 11 rounds,' he told *The Observer*, 'and come back. They want to see how far you will dig to get your goal.'

The Observer found Joshua staying in the accommodation used by Great Britain's amateur boxing squad in Sheffield, described as 'a cluttered sitting room-cum-kitchen in what appears to be a block of student accommodation'.

Joshua told Alex Clark, 'My new saying is, "I'm grinding like it's 2005."'

In 2005, Joshua was a teenage bricklayer, yet to lace on a pair of gloves.

By 2017, he was a multi-millionaire and arguably Britain's most recognisable sportsman, about to take part in the biggest heavyweight fight since Lennox Lewis humbled Mike Tyson in Memphis in 2002.

Lewis and Holyfield were there at the fight, along with Deontay Wilder – or should that be Beyonce Wilder?

Mischievous WBC cruiserweight champion Tony Bellew is one of the few with a personality as loud as Wilder's and when he spotted Wilder's name written on a ringside seat, he took a pen to it and renamed him.

The fight would be screened in 140 countries and for only the third time, rival American networks Showtime and HBO were both showing the fight.

This fight demanded the same interest as Lewis–Tyson and Floyd Mayweather Jr–Manny Pacquiao.

Sky Sports reported record pay-per-view buys for the latter fight, around 1.15 million, and hoped sales for Joshua–Klitschko would reach 1.5 million.

This was a fight that would sell without any pre-fight venom, so commonplace in recent big fights in Britain.

'I don't hate Klitschko, I don't hate Klitschko, I want to beat Klitschko,' Joshua told *The Guardian*.

Klitschko knew exactly how the fight was going to unfold. He told reporters during the final press conference he had recorded his prediction of the fight on to a USB stick and sewn it inside his dressing gown.

The gown and stick would be auctioned off after the fight.

The words just bounced off Joshua.

The following day, the public turned up in good numbers for the weigh-in at Wembley Arena and they saw Klitschko weigh 17st 2.25lb, the lightest he had been since beating Ruslan Chagaev more than eight years earlier, and Joshua scale a career-heaviest 17st 12lb.

These weights reinforced what most pundits were thinking. Joshua had trained for a short fight, Klitschko for a long one.

The following night, with 30 cameras beaming the fight around the world, Klitschko made his way to the ring to the familiarly funky twang of 'Don't Stop' by the Red Hot Chili Peppers and his face was etched in solemn concentration as he gently bounced on the balls of his feet while he waited for Joshua to make his entrance.

Klitschko had to wait several minutes. 'We wanted to showcase the crowd for TV,' explained Frank Smith, Matchroom's head of boxing, and throughout Joshua's lengthy entrance to the ring, Klitschko's gaze never left the canvas. Joshua was similarly focused when he reached the ring.

'I have never known a fighter being so still in the ring,' said Hearn of Joshua in the minutes before the opening bell.

'You don't really know if he is relaxed or if he is frozen. He crossed his hands and he didn't move.

'Then the mind games started from the Klitschkos and Vitali started staring him out. Joshua got wind of this and started staring Vitali out.

'I thought, "Don't do that, they want you to start burning energy."'

Despite the expectations, there was no explosive start from Joshua. Joshua told McCracken at the end of the opening round, 'Klitschko's hands seem really heavy,' and he was perhaps surprised by the length of his arms as well.

Klitschko did a good job of keeping Joshua on the outside in a quiet first round and the only clean punch of note in the second was a Klitschko right hand in the opening seconds that didn't bother Joshua. For the rest of the round, they jabbed and missed, feinted, tried to set traps.

There wasn't much between them in a quiet third as well before the fight really burst into life in the fourth.

For a few seconds, Joshua looked a bit disorganised after shipping a couple of rights early in the round and after his head cleared, he set about getting Klitschko back.

There was a slightly desperate look about some of Joshua's work and he didn't land cleanly with much, but with Klitschko not throwing much back, the round was surely his.

McCracken had noticed that at the start of every round, Klitschko let his right hand go. He told Joshua to get in first with his right hand in the fifth – and he did.

The punch landed and Klitschko wobbled, blood leaking from a wound on his left cheekbone. As Joshua kept the punches coming, Klitschko desperately tried to grab hold of him, but Joshua found the room, kept punching and Klitschko slid to his knees.

'In my heart of hearts, I thought I had him,' Joshua would later tell the BBC. 'I roared to the crowd as if I'd done it.'

The fight wasn't over. Klitschko got up quickly, but looked dazed and worse still, there was more than two minutes left in the round.

Joshua unloaded right hands and left hooks as the crowd screamed, but again, Klitschko was hard to nail flush and the flow of punches from Joshua slowed after Klitschko found his chin with a leaping left hook.

Only a clean punch from victory a minute or so earlier, incredibly, Joshua was now on rubbery legs. He grabbed, blocked and slipped as Klitschko, blood dripping from a wound under his left eyebrow, went after him.

Joshua tottered around the ring unsteadily, but he stayed upright until the bell and when it rang to signal the end of a dramatic round, he grinned. Joshua enjoys a good fight.

But this was a real crisis he was facing and at ringside, there were anxious faces.

'My mum [Susan] is a very, very pessimistic person,' said Hearn, 'and leaned over to me after the fifth round and said, "He [Joshua] is gone, he is gone."

'I said, "If he gets through the next two or three rounds, he is going to win this," and she just said, "No chance."'

Joshua grinned early in the sixth after blocking a Klitschko right hand – he knew that was the punch he was looking for – but moments later, it landed flush and Joshua went down.

Fortunately for Joshua, Klitschko missed with a left hook as he was falling, but still, he found himself on the seat of his trunks, tired and hurt. He started his rise at six, got up at seven and once the fight restarted, he had one minute and 40 seconds to get through until the bell.

Klitschko had Joshua in trouble, but there was no rush from the former champion.

He was content to take his time and wait for the openings to appear. Most of the punches he did throw missed and when he landed, Joshua grabbed. Joshua got through the round, but there seemed to be no way back for him.

Farhood, at ringside for American broadcasters Show-time, reckoned that at that point in the fight Joshua had 'about one chance in ten of winning. He looked exhausted and close to defeat.'

Vitali Klitschko told his brother in the corner after the sixth, 'Don't go forward, stay back, the guy is finished, you just have to wait.'

There was no urgency from Klitschko to finish the fight in the seventh and not many punches from Joshua.

Joshua's tongue was busy, however. He took a jab early in the round and then started talking to Klitschko, telling him, 'If you let me get through this round, I'm going to knock you the fuck out.'

That looked unlikely, but towards the end of a crisis-free seventh, there were signs Joshua was regaining energy.

He slipped a jab in the closing seconds and came back with a three-punch combination that lifted the spirits in his corner.

'He ain't got nothing left,' screamed McCracken. 'Come on mate, combinations!'

That proved beyond Joshua in the eighth, but there were jabs from him in a close round when not much happened.

McCracken wanted more from Joshua in the ninth. 'He's 41 and he's tired!' he shouted. 'Come on! Don't mess about!'

At the start of the ninth, as was the case at the start of most rounds, Klitschko let his right hand go. Twice. Joshua slipped the punch twice and smiled. Klitschko then got on the balls of his feet and started jabbing and moving with regularity.

Klitschko may well have won the round, but by its end, Joshua seemed re-energised and ready to push on in the closing three rounds.

After nine rounds, Joshua actually led on two of the scorecards, 86-83 and 86-85, and was a point down on the other.

The television commentators had Klitschko in a narrow lead and in Joshua's corner, McCracken tried to squeeze more out of his fighter.

McCracken felt Klitschko was trying to 'old man' Joshua out of the fight. That is, he thought Klitschko was using his experience to pinch close rounds. His tactic was to start rounds fast to leave Joshua chasing and then sit back and pick him off with jabs.

'You've got to get busy,' implored McCracken. 'You've got to press him and he won't stand up to it.'

Joshua put more into the tenth round without really troubling Klitschko – and made his breakthrough early in the 11th.

Joshua smacked Klitschko flush on the jaw with a right hand in the opening seconds of the round – and the punch shook him to his boots.

His legs stiffened, he grabbed hold of Joshua and when they were separated, Klitschko got on his toes.

'I'm looking at him thinking, "Is he hurt?"' remembered Joshua, '"because I don't want to waste any energy here." I thought, "Eff this."'

Joshua went for Klitschko, couldn't catch him and after 30 seconds or so, Klitschko was back standing his ground in the centre of the ring and apparently fully recovered.

Joshua fired a right hand, then a left hook. Klitschko got underneath both punches and the position Joshua found himself in, the only punch he could throw next was a right uppercut.

The shot struck Klitschko under the chin with tremendous force, knocking his head back and dazing him.

This looked like a huge moment in the fight.

Klitschko appeared ragged once more and Joshua pounced, throwing left-rights at him until he ended up on his knees in a corner.

Klitschko got up needing to soak up a few seconds to help his head clear – but he didn't get them. Joshua was straight on him. He found the target with another right hand that kept Klitschko in trouble and Joshua hunted him down to the ropes.

His straight left-rights were blocked and he quickly had a rethink, launching a right uppercut that found its way through Klitschko's defences and on to his chin. Joshua quickly followed it with a left hook and Klitschko went crashing again.

This time he took several seconds to convince referee David Fields he was fit to continue after getting to his feet, but once the fight restarted, it was clear there were to be no further twists and the fight was now Joshua's.

He pinned Klitschko in a corner, furiously threw his fists at him and after a few seconds, the referee jumped in to stop the fight.

Joshua savoured the few seconds he had to himself before he was engulfed by his trainers and Hearn, while at ringside, Klitschko's partner, Hayden Panettiere, wept uncontrollably as millions of viewers around the world watched on.

The *Daily Star on Sunday*'s front-page headline screamed 'Fight of the Century' and the *Sunday Mirror* was in agreement.

'It was an astonishing battle,' wrote Andy Dunn, and Nick Greenslade in the *Sunday Times* wrote of 'one of the great nights in British boxing'.

'What I learned about myself in that fight,' Joshua would say later, 'was that I have the deep-down character that no one can teach you in training.

'When you're up against someone who can match you punch for punch, power for power and speed for speed, it becomes [about] who you are and how bad you want it.

'That fight was everything I'd trained for in the last eight years.

'Forget everything else, it was mano-a-mano. This was me and Klitschko, this was about pride.

'When it comes to boxing, I just strip it back to reality and focus on what it really is. It's just me and a man coming to blows – and the best man will win.'

'The fight went beyond everyone's expectations,' said Farhood.

'If you were writing a script, you couldn't have written it any better.

'That was, in many ways, the best performance of Klitschko's career. He enhanced his reputation more that night than in all his wins and as for Joshua, everyone now wants to see his next fight.'

Asked the following day what was next, Joshua answered, 'Do what Klitschko did next.

'Maintain, maintain, maintain. That's important. It's good to achieve it now, but what would be better for me is to just maintain it. That's what I said to Klitschko. For me, it's not a defining fight. It's just part of my journey.

'What more can we do? And how long can we do it? That's what I find interesting.'

Fight No 20
Carlos Takam

At: Principality Stadium, Cardiff

On: Saturday, 28 October 2017

Opponent's record: Fights 39 Wins 35 Losses 3 Draws 1

Joshua's weight: 18st 2lb

Opponent's weight: 16st 11.5lb

Scheduled for: 12 Rounds

IBF heavyweight title, WBA Super world heavyweight title

Result: Joshua won by tenth-round stoppage

HIS WIN over Klitschko, every writer and fan's fight of the year, made Joshua possibly the most high-profile fighter in the world and left Obisia Nwankpa with some explaining to do.

The Sun discovered that a decade previously, Nigerian boxing coaches had told Joshua he wasn't good enough to represent the country of his parents' birth.

'Joshua was in Nigeria once to connect with his roots and I think that was in 2007,' explained Jeremiah Okorodudu, a quarter-finalist at the Los Angeles Olympics in 1984.

'He wanted a chance to compete for trials ahead of the 2008 Beijing Olympics, but he was denied and not given a chance.'

Nwankpa was the coach who made the decision. 'We made the right call then,' he explained, 'because he wasn't good enough and we sent someone much better.'

Onorede Ehwareme represented Nigeria at super-heavyweight in Beijing – and lost his first bout there.

The temptation is to think Joshua would have fared much better, but at the time he asked for a trial with the Nigerian coaches, he hadn't even boxed competitively.

Nigeria still backed him and when he fought Klitschko, thousands gathered in Joshua's father's home town, Sagamu, around 40 miles from capital city Lagos, to watch.

Celebrations after 'Femi' triumphed lasted into the early hours.

Hearn said in the aftermath of the Klitschko victory that a fight in Nigeria was possible.

'Joshua Wants To Tour the World Just Like Ali' read the headline in *The Times* and possible venues included China, Nigeria, Dubai and, of course, America.

America was looking forward to seeing him. 'Joshua has the potential to be the biggest man in sport, not just boxing,' said Steve Farhood days after the Klitschko fight.

'He's not just a good-looking heavyweight with a punch, he understands it's about what you do outside the ring as well.

'With fighters like Jack Dempsey, Joe Louis and Muhammad Ali, the heavyweight champion stood for something bigger than just the title and we have lost that in recent years.

'To get as big as them, Joshua needs playmates – and the obvious one is [WBC champion] Deontay Wilder.

'The Wilder fight needs a US pay-per-view audience and to get that, Joshua needs exposure in the States.

'We need to see him in the States. Joshua still hasn't fought over here and if he wants the recognition Floyd Mayweather and Manny Pacquiao have had, he needs to fight in Las Vegas.'

That was the plan, for Joshua to fight Klitschko in a rematch in Las Vegas on 11 November.

Joshua, along with Hearn, Freddie Cunningham, Joshua's commercial manager, and Frank Smith, head of Matchroom Boxing, headed to Vegas to talk about the possibility of staging the fight at the T-Mobile Arena.

Stephen Espinoza, Showtime Sports executive vice-president and general manager, described the Joshua–Klitschko rematch as 'the biggest heavyweight Vegas fight in a couple of decades.

'It's a mega fight, wherever it is.'

It's a mega fight that didn't happen.

Klitschko announced in August that he was retiring from boxing, leaving journalists to decide his place in the sport's history, and Joshua with mixed emotions.

'In some ways I'm glad there isn't going to be a second fight between me and Klitschko because it would have dampened what happened the first time if the rematch wasn't as thrilling or exciting,' he explained.

'But then for the love of the sport I would have loved to fight him again.

'People said Klitschko was too old, but I knew they were wrong because his mind was in the right place and, like he said, he was obsessed about getting his titles back.

'Floyd Mayweather is still firing at 40, even though he has had a career having to make weight, which means he's had to starve his body of certain nutrients and has never been able to develop properly.

'Klitschko is the same age as Mayweather, he doesn't have to worry about the weight and has fed his body with the best food.

'Heavyweights develop at a later stage and Klitschko had dominated for a long time, so I thought he would come again because I knew he still had the fighter left in him.

'It was the opportunity for us to go to the States and that's kind of what let me down.'

The retirement of Klitschko at least meant Joshua could fulfil his obligations to the IBF.

They were insisting he should defend against his mandatory challenger, Kubrat Pulev, by 2 December and had he fought Klitschko instead, there was the possibility the IBF would have stripped him of their belt. Hearn would have surely attempted to smooth the situation over by offering Pulev some step-aside money, but as it turned out, that wouldn't be necessary.

Joshua would fight Pulev at the Principality Stadium in Cardiff on Saturday, 28 October and Matchroom reported that within 24 hours of tickets going on sale, 75,000 had been sold.

Tickets would possibly have sold just as well had the fight taken place in Bulgaria.

Pulev was a hero there, a former Beijing Olympian and European heavyweight champion whose profile was raised by his relationship with singer Andrea Teodora.

The only blemish on Pulev's record was a crushing five-round loss to Wladimir Klitschko in a world title challenge in November 2014. Solid wins over Dereck Chisora, Samuel Peter and Kevin Johnson propelled Pulev back up the rankings and into championship contention.

He was surely the most skilled opponent Joshua had yet to face, but according to those well placed to judge, he lacked the size and punch to beat Joshua.

'Joshua has too much for him,' said Matt Skelton, who fought both. 'He's too strong, too athletic – and he punches too hard.'

In the weeks leading up to the fight, there were rumours Pulev was going to pull out of the fight through injury.

His promoters, the German-based Sauerland brothers, made no comment and then 12 days before the fight, the announcement was made that because of a torn pectoral muscle, Pulev would not be fighting Joshua.

That left Hearn and Joshua with a decision to make. Either they cancelled the show or they found another opponent.

Neither wanted a cancellation and Joshua suggested a rematch with Dillian Whyte.

Whyte had come back with five straight wins following defeat in their first fight a couple of years ago and was training to fight on the undercard in Cardiff.

He was matched with giant former European champion Robert Helenius, but the IBF insisted Joshua should face the next highest ranked challenger.

Joshua had met Carlos Takam before.

'He came to my fight against Dominic Breazeale at the O2 Arena last year and waited for me in the reception of my hotel,' remembered Joshua.

'He came over to me and said, "I want to fight you" and I said, "I've just had a fight."

'But I knew who he was.'

Joshua also knew the 36-year-old was 'incredibly durable', adding at a press conference, 'This guy's head is like a block of cement. He's so tough, he just keeps walking forward.

'So let's see what fire he's ready to walk through.'

Takam had been around for a while and was well respected within the trade. He represented Cameroon at the 2004 Olympics in Athens and had fought in good company since turning professional, basing himself in France with the Cherchi family.

Takam had been in and around the world's top ten heavyweights ever since drawing with Cuban southpaw Mike Perez in 2014 and also had a good win over capable American Tony Thompson.

But at the highest level, Takam had been knocked out by Alexander Povetkin and outpointed by Joseph Parker.

The Parker fight was competitive and Takam didn't do enough in too many of the rounds.

At around 6ft 1in, Takam was around three inches shorter than Pulev and had a rolling-and-hooking style that had made him an ideal sparring partner for David Haye ahead of his grudge fight with Dereck Chisora at West Ham United's Upton Park ground in July 2012.

Looking through the fighter's records, reporters noticed Reading veteran Michael Sprott had fought both Joshua and Takam and sought out his opinion.

Sprott, beaten in the first round by Joshua when he was on the way up and the fifth round by Takam a few months later, told them Takam had a chance, if he could get through the opening few rounds.

The longer the fight went, Sprott reckoned, the better it was for Takam.

'He's very strong,' said Sprott of the challenger. 'He can definitely take a shot.

'Before, he [Joshua] was fighting someone who was 6ft 4in. Now he's fighting someone who is 6ft 1in.

'And remember when Lennox Lewis fought Vitali Klitschko [in 2003], he was meant to be fighting someone else [Kirk Johnson] and Lennox probably should have lost that fight.'

Lewis was behind on all three scorecards when Klitschko was ruled out after six rounds with eye damage.

Historians also remembered journeyman 'Smokin'' Bert Cooper stepping in at short notice to hand Evander Holyfield the first count of his professional career in an unlikely world title challenge before losing in seven rounds.

Though the bookmakers didn't seem to think so, there was a chance this could be a difficult night for Joshua.

The Independent's headline on the day of the fight read, 'Takam is a tougher nut for Joshua to crack than many think' and Steve Bunce wrote underneath it that the challenger 'took the fight at short notice, is a long way short of peak, but an equal distance from being the sacrificial lamb of some perverted narratives'.

Bunce felt that had Takam been given 12 weeks to prepare then he would have lasted the distance, but at only 12 days' notice, he predicted a Joshua win inside six rounds.

Joshua knew both the importance of beating Takam – possible unification fights with Deontay Wilder and Joseph Parker were at stake – and also the importance of beating him well.

The Klitschko fight hadn't convinced everyone and those who were convinced, Joshua was keen to impress once more.

Joshua accepted if he didn't win well, 'People will think, "Oooh, he isn't as good as we thought or he won't be as good as we think he will be,"' and he wanted to keep the public behind him.

After a public training session to publicise the fight, Gareth A. Davies wrote in *The Telegraph* that Joshua had the same sort of grip on his public that Muhammad Ali once had.

Joshua himself knew he wasn't universally popular. 'My picture is on billboards everywhere,' he wrote in *Boxing News*, 'and I think, any girl I've ever dated, their boyfriend must hate me. He's going in the gym and seeing my face everywhere.

'But none of them [the billboards] were really up until after the Klitschko fight.'

That was the fight that made Joshua a huge star and he knew that should he struggle with Takam, the victory over Klitschko would be tarnished.

If the Takam fight was hard, there were those who would say Joshua only beat Klitschko because Klitschko was old.

Joshua himself wasn't happy with his performance against Klitschko.

'That fight wasn't just the best thing that happened to heavyweight boxing,' said sparring partner Frazer Clarke, 'it was the best thing to happen to Joshua too. He's woken up. He was shocking in that fight, absolutely terrible, and he admits it.'

Clarke noticed Joshua 'thinking more' during spars.

Pulev was a thinking fighter, a smart technician who boxed on the balls of his feet, but Joshua instead ended up facing a solid opponent who was known for fighting with a tank-like aggression.

Joshua didn't want to give ground to Takam and once the change of opponent was announced, he piled on a few extra pounds.

The day before the fight, Joshua weighed in at a career-heaviest, hard-to-budge 18st 2lb, with Takam at 16st 11.5lb.

There was no animosity between the fighters at the weigh-in, only an awkward-looking handshake.

There was a solid look about Takam, but he was small and had been around for long enough to know he was in for a hard night. There were no bold predictions from the challenger. He just said he was 'a winner' and always went into fights believing he would win.

The following night, Joshua went largely unnoticed by the 78,000 crowd when he made his way to the ring.

The entrance of possibly the most famous boxer in the world fell rather flat as the lighting and sound systems both failed.

Pundits wondered ahead of the opening bell whether Takam would take the fight to Joshua, go for broke.

He didn't. He stayed on the outside, looking to slip Joshua's punches and jump in with right hands and left hooks when the openings were there.

Joshua was purposeful and at the same time watchful. Takam was a difficult, moving, target and there was weight behind his counter punches.

Early in the second, Takam jumped in and heads clashed, leaving Joshua with his nose swollen and bleeding, possibly broken.

'It was like getting hit in the face with a brick,' was how McCracken described the impact.

Joshua tried to blink away the pain and encouraged, Takam unloaded. Joshua stood with Takam and blasted him with a left hook that had him looking unsteady and he went on the back foot for the remainder of the round.

The third was a quieter session and Joshua made a breakthrough in the fourth, slicing open a gash on Takam's right eyebrow.

Blood ran down the side of his face. It looked like the end of the fight.

Referee Phil Edwards had a look at the wound and asked Takam if he should wave the fight off.

Takam shook his head, waded into Joshua and shipped a left hook during an exchange that sent him reeling back. His glove touched the floor and he took an eight count.

The 15 seconds left in the round weren't enough for Joshua to finish the fight.

There were concerns for Takam at the end of the round. Edwards went to his corner to look at his eye and the challenger confirmed he wanted to carry on fighting.

Still, the cut on his right eyebrow was severe enough for the referee to ask the ringside doctor for his opinion. He said Takam could continue and once the fight restarted, Takam started to take more risks. But whenever they exchanged, Joshua had the tighter defence and the heavier hands and it was Takam who had to give ground.

Boxing News editor Matt Christie compared the sound of Joshua's punches landing to 'water melons being cannoned into a brick wall' and to the surprise and admiration of ringsiders, Takam kept taking them, kept trying to find a way to win the fight.

He got through the first half of the fight, if only just, and then wanted to push on and try to win it.

Takam started to unload more punches in the seventh round and ended up shipping more punishment.

Joshua opened a cut over his left eye and there was another sequence later in the round that might have disheartened a fighter with less spirit than Takam.

Joshua shook his head after Takam let his hands go, then dropped his hands by his sides contemptuously and unloaded with a two-fisted counter attack that left Takam on shaky legs for a few seconds.

The burst left Joshua short of breath. For the final minute or so of the seventh, his mouth hung open and he took a break from punching Takam and started talking to him instead.

Neither fighter threw much until the last minute of the ninth when Joshua opened up and crashed a left hook off Takam's jaw.

Again, the punch didn't budge him and at the start of the tenth, Takam took the fight to Joshua.

He kept his hands up to block the hooks being flung at him and then found the target with a short, jolting right uppercut that made Takam's body shake.

The predator in Joshua told him that his opponent was 'ready to go', as fighters say, and he got through with enough punches in the following few seconds to convince the referee to stop the fight.

As Edwards stepped between the fighters, Takam started to fire back, but his retaliation came a second or two too late.

Edwards had made up his mind and the fight was over. Takam protested, but blood leaked from both eyes, he had shipped a lot of punishment and didn't have the punch to wipe out the points deficit on the scorecards.

For the first time in his career, Joshua heard the crowd's boos at the end of a fight. They had come to see Joshua knock someone out and he shared their dissatisfaction. He had come to knock someone out.

'I think people want to see Takam unconscious on the floor,' Joshua said during the post-fight press conference. 'That's where I was trying to get to.'

That wasn't the ending the referee wanted.

There were those who criticised the stoppage out of sympathy to Takam. The feeling was that having taken and given so much, he deserved to hear the final bell if possible.

He didn't hear the final bell and by making a successful fourth defence of the IBF title, Joshua made history.

No other British heavyweight had achieved that and the next target was to unify the titles.

'[WBC champion] Deontay Wilder versus Anthony Joshua has to happen,' said Hearn.

'Deontay Wilder will be relieved of that belt in 2018.'

Anthony Joshua
Professional Record

2013

Oct 5 Emanuele Leo w rsc 1 Greenwich 16st 6lb 12ozs

Oct 26 Paul Butlin w rsc 2 Sheffield 16st 8lb 8oz

Nov 14 Hrvoje Kisicek w rsc 2 Bethnal Green 16st 5lb

2014

Feb 1 Dorian Darch w rsc 2 Cardiff 17st 3lb 8oz

Mar 1 Hector Alfredo Avila w ko 1 Glasgow 17st

May 31 Matt Legg w ko 1 Wembley Stadium 16st 12lb

Jul 12 Matt Skelton w rsc 2 Liverpool 17st 1lb

Sep 13 Konstantin Airich w rsc 3 Manchester 17st 2lb 8oz

Oct 11 Denis Bakhtov w rsc 2 Greenwich 16st 12lb 8oz
[Vacant WBC International heavyweight title]

Nov 22 Michael Sprott w rsc 1 Liverpool 17st 2lb
[Eliminator, British heavyweight title]

2015

Apr 4 Jason Gavern w ko 3 Newcastle 17st 7lb

May 9 Raphael Zumbano Love w rsc 2 Birmingham 17st
10lb

May 30 Kevin Johnson w rsc 2 Greenwich 17st 10lb 8oz
[WBC International heavyweight title]

Sep 12 Gary Cornish w rsc 1 Greenwich 17st 11lb
[Vacant Commonwealth heavyweight title, WBC
International heavyweight title]

Dec 12 Dillian Whyte w rsc 7 Greenwich 17st 7lb
[Commonwealth heavyweight title, vacant British
heavyweight title, WBC International heavyweight title]

2016

Apr 9 Charles Martin w ko 2 Greenwich 17st 6lb
[IBF heavyweight title]

Jun 25 Dominic Breazeale w rsc 7 Greenwich 17st 5lb
[IBF heavyweight title]

Dec 10 Eric Molina w rsc 3 Manchester 17st 11lb
[IBF heavyweight title]

2017

Apr 29 Wladimir Klitschko w rsc 11 Wembley Stadium 17st 12lb
[IBF heavyweight title, WBA Super world heavyweight title]

Oct 28 Carlos Takam w rsc 10 Cardiff 18st 2lb
[IBF heavyweight title, WBA Super world heavyweight title]

2018

Mar 31 Joseph Parker w pts 12 Cardiff 17st 4¼lbs

(IBF heavyweight title, WBA Super world heavyweight title,
WBO heavyweight title)

Fights 21 Wins 21

Index